THE AETHER: CRADLE OF CREATION

AND VITAL TO ALL LIFE

By George E Moss

"Facts do not cease to exist because they are ignored."
—Aldous Huxley

"When science begins the study of non-physical phenomena,
it will make more progress in one decade than in all the
centuries of its experience."
—Fred Hoyle

CONTENTS

CW01507601

ACKNOWLEDG

For many years, George's books h
the words of Salumet have been co............
a task which George, *(my father)* undertook humbly and with
earnestness and sincerity. *(His middle name is Ernest!)*
Deepest thanks to the *very dedicated* team, past and present,
of what has come to be known as the *'Salumet Circle'*.
Special thanks to Graham, who used his decades of experience
teaching science, to check through the manuscript—
fortunately all the science got full marks from the teacher!
Deepest thanks of course to Eileen, the dedicated full-trance
channel to Salumet. This circle is truly a team, all playing an
integral part in this *spiritual family*, which has its counterparts
in *Spirit realm*, including *gatekeepers, guides, helpers* and
others of whom we may not even be aware.

Thank you all!

To see a rare filmed session of the Salumet Circle, here's a
Link: https://www.youtube.com/watch?v=1hBIXN3nwjs
Alternatively, use your phone to scan the QR code:

FOREWORD

In the summer of 1989, with dear wife Ann, George joined his two sons Mark and Paul, visiting the Mayan pyramids of Mexico—a most illuminating experience, guiding George to the *'Salumet Circle'* with the truly exceptional Light Being known as Salumet. George's expertise in logical scientific inquiry became invaluable as Salumet's mission unfolded— just as the microscopes in George's labs revealed material evidence, his forensic skills now focus like a *spiritual microscope*, highlighting deeper truths of existence.

In this book, George examines the mysterious Aether as a precursor to material universe formation and essential to all life-forms. It may sound complex, but both George and Salumet are able to express deep matters in beautifully simple terms.

Over the years I have received regular transcripts of the meetings, originally from George and now from Paul. I have always looked forward to these, especially when Salumet was speaking, as it was always words of *Truth* and *wisdom* and always re-assuring. There have also been some wonderful rescues and guided meditations which add a richness to my life.

William Roache OBE

PREFACE

It is a great honour to have been asked to write a preface to George's final book.

I am not a scientist and if he wasn't my father-in-law, we perhaps wouldn't have met. Having said that, his open-mindedness and his microscopic lenses on the spiritual, made us closer than one could imagine.

George is a great storyteller; he knows how to put science into "understandable" language, always searching for Salumet's confirmation that he is on the right track, bending his mind in all sorts of directions—he just loved that kind of mind-gymnastics!

If you are familiar with George's work, you should be familiar with Salumet's as well—this conglomerate or union of non-physical beings from across multiple universes have written the books hand-in-hand, one on Earth, one in Spirit—a lovely team.

Eileen has been channelling Salumet since 1994. We are incredibly fortunate and grateful to receive these *teachings* via a *full-trance* medium, which means the *ego* is placed to one side, allowing the *purest* possible connection.

I hope that you will love this book as I have.

Love and Light—always,
Sabine Moss

INTRODUCTION

As a free-thinking scientist who now sits with a leading séance group guided by one from Angelic Realms, I feel highly privileged. But whilst boldly sampling the benefits of both worlds, I also feel very much a nonconformist. Throughout the 20th century, our mainstream scientific community has been so devoted to *material*—that is entirely *physical* constructs that any scientific *paranormal* studies have met with serious suspicion. In fact, what is termed paranormal has been defined as *beyond the scope of normal scientific understanding*—or one might say: beyond *physical* explanation—a dismissive statement that in effect rejects all that goes on within a séance group. Of course, peer-reviewed journals publish the research of mainstream institutions and not that of séance groups. But lack of review by mainstream journals is fast becoming of less consequence since the Internet now rapidly expands to become *the* major source of information exchange—all part of a rapidly changing world.

A brief outline of the work of the Salumet Circle is relevant here and will help to illustrate the above development. All weekly meetings of the group for nearly three decades have been recorded and transcribed with the utmost care—transmissions received from spirit amounting to literally millions of words. The gathering together of numerous threads of valuable data from this and from other key sources has then followed. By connecting together so many separately sourced facts it has been possible to see so much more clearly some of the patterns within this complex and wonderful creation. The *spiritual sources* of information involved in this study include light-beings from Angelic Realms and several *well-progressed* knowledgeable ones that now continue their journeys in spirit. *Non-spirit* sources of information include: philosophers from Earth's ancient past, more recent scientific material (mainstream science plus recent remarkable pyramid energy studies) and important input from the most amazing sentient extraterrestrial beings with whom we have been privileged to meet during séance evenings. A point that should be made at this early stage is this: I do indeed acknowledge and respect the forays of our mainstream scientists—not least because I have been one myself! Sometimes they are correct, sometimes not. Errors in the scientific literature that may take more than a little time to sort out are inevitable; that is to be expected, as all strive to probe the unknown. The detailed data from experiment has much more than just its prima facie value. Such data provides the basis for further discussion with others, who may have vastly differing experience. Our group is indeed fortunate in having knowledgeable friends in spirit who communicate, as well as friends out there across the universe.

Before getting down to details, a brief overview of what might be seen as a general threefold basis of existence should help us to see how the 'aether' has its place within the grand pattern of creation. So let us describe those three major components—beginning with spirit:

SPIRIT: This part of the universe might be described as truly universal as well as time-less. Although spirit has within itself no spatial factor, or has no *recognition* of space, it nevertheless is everywhere. It may be difficult to think spiritually and get one's head around this concept! But it is a fact that spirit has no recognition of space yet is all-pervading. Although space-less, we may think of spirit as the home of a number of different non-physical entities—Angelic light-beings, ascended masters, progressing souls and soul aspects—the latter having experienced planetary life, with likely reincarnation involving *many* planetary lives. We may also think of spirit as the abode of mind, thought, consciousness, prayer and telepathic communications. And it is the *energy* of spirit that embodies the fundamental Creative Principle/Creative Force that powers everything ultimately into material existence.

AETHER: This part of existence is also truly universal. In the creation process, there has to be an intermediate stage between spirit and the material world with which we are all so familiar, and the aether is precisely that intermediate stage. Unlike our material world, the aether is not based on atoms and molecules yet it continues to be a vital factor in our lives—we simply could not live without it. This becomes clearly evident if we consider that aether is the conducting medium for all electromagnetic (EM) wave-forms—sunlight, starlight, radio, TV, mobile phone etc. In addition to being the pre-cursor of material universe formation, aether is essential to its upkeep—to the upkeep of the entire cosmos and essential to all life forms that continue within it. This will become clear in due process, and in any event all life forms need the sunlight that it conveys.

THE MATERIALIZED UNIVERSE: Planet Earth and all the visible material cosmos are comprised of atoms and molecules, plus of course their smaller components such as ions and electrons. All are derived *from* the aether—from that half-way stage of creation so to speak. Here on Earth, our developed senses have instant awareness of nature's living structures, while beyond Earth we can at night appreciate the extreme beauty of the heavens. Our brains belong to the material creation but their function does not end there. Brains also have wonderful connections via mind—mind can reach out beyond brain and go far in telepathic union. Each of us is so much more than *just* one material being; there are the connections via aether and there are our links to spirit, which must not ever be overlooked. All life relies upon the sunlight and those other EM-waves that ride on the aether medium. And we all enjoy from our spirit connections—guidance via intuition, dream-state, synchronicity; and there is that very necessary spiritual rejuvenation every night during sleep-state. Mind returns to spirit during that regular sleep state and we awaken refreshed.

Reference has already been made to our mainstream science. Some names are well remembered for the enlightenment of their intuition and ingenuity; such names as Plato and

Aristotle have stood the test of time. In more recent years Sir Isaac Newton, James Clerk Maxwell and Albert Einstein have helped us on our continuing journey into what present day humanity describes as 'the unknown'. But not all scientists have received the acclaim that they deserve, and perhaps the casual reader will not have come across Nikolai Kozyrev—his valuable contributions towards proving aether existence will be mentioned as we move on. The progress, or knowledge of that progress, has sometimes faltered on account of wayward politics, or sometimes it has just taken a little time for the penny to drop—for new ideas to gain acceptance. Such has been the course of our more recent Earthly progress.

PART 1 – EARLY PHILOSOPHY VERSUS MODERN SCIENCE

CHAPTER 1 – THE GREEKS AND EASTERN EMERGENCE

M nesarchus and his wife Parthenis had travelled to the Greek city of Delphi, famed for its oracle dedicated to Apollo. There, before returning to Syria, they had consulted the Prophetess (a 'medium' in modern séance group parlance) through whom Apollo speaks. To their utter astonishment, his words uttered via the Prophetess—the Pythia—ignored the question placed and informed them of Parthenis' pregnancy; stating that their son would be a man of much wisdom from whom the world would benefit. It was a revelation that took them both completely by surprise; and in due process the lady indeed begat a son. And it very soon became clear that he was to be one of unquestionable wisdom. Some authors have since observed parallels between their son and the coming of Jesus—each birth having been predicted, a *ghost-figure* having appeared to Mnesarchus to instruct against their union during the pregnancy, each would receive Divine inspiration and each would become known as 'Son of God'. [In the much later

Roman times it was always the teaching of the learned Arius that Jesus was *a son* who was in receipt of Divine inspiration. Quite so; but this description of Jesus was not accepted by the man-made state-religions that followed. The significance of this important point will be explained as we progress.] So this briefly is how PYTHAGORAS (circa 590-490 BC) came into the world, and the world has most certainly benefited from his endeavours.

Travelling far, Pythagoras became conversant with the variously styled *mystery schools* of his day. Previously, wise men had often been referred to as 'sages', meaning 'those who know'. As a man of propriety and intelligence Pythagoras changed that. He coined the term 'philosopher', with the slightly different meaning of 'one who is attempting to find out'. Self-styled thus, he became this world's first philosopher, and he established a school of philosophy at Crotona, Southern Italy. At the age of sixty, he married one of his disciples there and they raised seven children. Pythagoras carried his age extremely well, staying active and remaining in good health, very nearly reaching one hundred years. But then, as with Jesus, he also was senselessly murdered by those who disagreed—a further similarity. But his teachings have lived on and his name is still revered by many in the world today. Those teachings of course embrace subtleties of mathematics—the intricacies of solid geometry, including pyramid, diamond and dodecahedral shapes that are significant forms embodied in the material creation. And there is of course his 'Pythagoras theorem' concerning the special properties of right-angle triangles—the square of the hypotenuse always equalling the sum of squares of the other two sides.

In Greece at that time, the world was considered to be based on four elements—earth, air, fire and water. We would more aptly class these today as four states of matter that the now more extensive and better-known elements are known to comprise—but it was a reasoned and acceptable beginning. Pythagoras was the first to consider that 'aether' should be seen as a *fifth element*—thought of then as a pure fresh air breathed by the gods. Plato and Aristotle came on the scene a little more than 100-years later and extended the thinking. Plato saw aether as *framing* the tangible universe—excellent! Aristotle, student of Plato, declared this encompassing fifth element to exhibit no properties within its self. It does not get hot or cold for example as do earth, air, fire and water.

We have mentioned gods and the Oracle. Many will say: 'All Rubbish! It is mere mythology and the gods of the Greeks are of no import in today's world.' This I have to say is most assuredly not so! In fact, highly significant communications from those Angelic Realms, for the benefit and guidance of today's world, continue still, and some of those recent communications have related to our mythical past and to the gods of Greece. I will explain: the one from Angelic Realms that we know as 'Salumet' has been guide and teacher to the Salumet Circle, for the last 30 years. The ongoing mission has been to teach *truth of existence*. All commentaries have been published in several books and website: www.salumetandfriends.org. Salumet's following statements

13

(9th July 2007) concerning those Angelic Beings of this and other planets should help to clarify this particular topic:

~ **"The Angelic Beings from all other planets are working hard to help humankind and it is a little unfortunate perhaps, that the people of this time have lost that knowledge and consciousness of your ancient peoples. It would be worthwhile, my dear friends, if you would strive to attain just a little of that consciousness which the ancients had. They, of course, were able to *see* these Angelic Beings but they called them in your mythology 'gods', and although they may have seemed liked gods because of their great knowledge and help, they are in fact the Angelic Beings which have always been a part of this Earth planet."**

In reply to that, I had suggested that it has been our tendency in past times to refer to *any* who are not human and who seem greater than humans, as 'gods'.

~ **"Yes. After all, remember *you* are gods in your own right because we are all from the same source. But of course I feel you would think that not possible—but your actual substance is from the Great Creative Force. That is why in all of your religions mankind claims to be part of that god-like energy. So I say to you my dear friends, strive forwards to achieve evermore spiritual consciousness in your daily lives in order that those spiritual eyes be awakened to all that is round and about you. Be part of the whole."**

14

So, the ancient Greek mythology must never be dismissed as fanciful; it is neither conjecture nor fiction. It is meaningful fact, and Zeus and the gods of Olympus are in today's language 'Angelic Beings'. Equally, Homer, writing in even earlier times included visible 'gods' in the scenes of his *Odyssey* and *Iliad*. It seems that it would have been natural for him to include these as visible entities in the Earthly scenes that he described. And then later, Apollo from Angelic Realms spoke via the entranced Delphi Pythia to accurately predict the coming of Pythagoras. Quite so; and by the same token, Salumet from Angelic Realms now regularly speaks via the entranced medium Eileen Roper during meetings of the Salumet |Circle—not for the purpose of predicting Earthly events, although this does occasionally happen during the wonderful ongoing meetings that we are privileged to have.

[Please note that I am not declaring how much of Homer's stories are fact or how much fiction. I simply state that it would have been natural for him to include the participation of visible Angelic Beings in those stories and for him to refer to them as 'gods'. This in itself is of course an important realization for the present-day student of Homeric literature.]

It is appropriate that we name one other Angelic Being at this stage of our investigation. His name is 'Zabdiel' and I mentioned him to Salumet at our meeting of 12th May 2014:
Q: "I have been reading recently Salumet, about a wonderful spirit of the name
'Zabdiel', who spoke through the Rev George Vale-Owen in the year 1913, and he described his place in spirit as 'Sphere

15

10'; so I think he is a fairly well advanced one in spirit. Much of what he says is in line with what you have told us."

~ "He is one of the Angelic Group."

I had responded: "Ah! He is Angelic!" and our guide readily confirmed this indeed to be so.

Moving on from those early Greek philosophers, Plotinus (205-270) added further constructive thought. Plotinus was born Egyptian and followed Ammonius of Alexandria— Alexandria having become an intellectual centre of the world. Plotinus later moved on to Rome where he furthered and taught philosophy from which many would benefit. The fourth treatise of his 'Second Ennead' is headed *'Matter in its Two Kinds'*. Here he reasons from first principles that matter must exist in two different kinds. That which is familiar to us as 'material world' has form and is of a shifting time-bound nature. But where could it have come from? He reasoned that there has to be a pre-existing matter that is void of all form and this pre-existing matter must also have a source. He therefore reasons a link to the 'Primal-Principles', and indicates the sequence: Creative Principle > formless matter (aether) > shifting matter with its visible forms (material world).

This overall pattern of creation and the 5-element classification had then remained with Earth with only slight variation for hundreds of years—being cited in Hindu and Buddhist religions and in the Tibetan Bön philosophy. There followed the Medieval alchemy, developed mainly by the

Persian alchemist Jäbir ibn Hayyän (circa 721-815); the 'elements' listed in his day being earth, air, fire, water, sulphur and mercury. Little else of note occurred until after the European 'black death' followed by the 'renaissance'. Then Europe seemed to come alive in a very material but nevertheless logical sense, with development of the scientific method based on experiment and observed empirical evidence. Many Earthly names are remembered in this context and some of them would make handsome contribution to the knowledge held in certain branches of science connecting with that so called mysterious fifth element—the aether.

CHAPTER 2 – PROCEDURAL MEASURES AND PAST ERRORS

S o before moving on to more modern and more familiar achievements, how shall we best proceed? It might be well if we clarify a few points about the procedures that we are about to follow:

In view of the enormous and increasing numbers of names in the scientific annals one cannot possibly name all without seriously overwhelming the reader. But let me make it clear here and now that the contributions of *all* have helped humanity on our forward journey. It is therefore appropriate to make it clear that *all* are appreciated and thanked for their contributions.

In the interest of brevity just first and last names of those involved will usually be cited.

I shall standardise with the 'aether' spelling, with apologies to publishers who have opted for the 'ether' spelling for their presentations (but 'ether' is of course also a term used to denote the anaesthetic 'diethyl ether'; the original 'aether' spelling therefore avoids ambiguity).

The term 'space-time' will be used to denote Einstein's 4-dimentional concept that comprises 3-dimensional space plus time as a fourth dimension.

I do not intend to digress into mathematical processes. Do I hear sighs of relief? But that is not to say that the work of adept mathematicians is not treasured—it is, and very much so. And brilliant discoveries have resulted from such excursions. That being so, how then shall we argue the case for aether as an essential part of this universe and essential to all planetary life; and how do we demonstrate its connections to matter in its entirety? I propose to use (1) reference to historic record, (2) a process of simple logical deduction, (3) interdisciplinary comparisons, (4) facts derived from extraterrestrial sentient beings of greater knowledge than ourselves, (5) guidance from unquestionable spirit sources, and of course (6) certain quite recent Earthly disclosures made by our scientists that ring true. I also intend to be so bold as to point out where mainstream science is currently in error and has been in obvious error in the past. And it is of course always so much easier to look back and see error in retrospect. There have certainly been a number of huge errors made through history that we can now look back on—not just in science but also in the more general sense. Perhaps 'blunder' is a better word than error, and when sufficient time has elapsed each blunder becomes crystal clear in retrospect. The first step in a society that dares to be self-analytical is to deduce and accept that humans have indeed made blunders; also that each false step has often required a surprising amount of time for recognition. But we need to become accustomed to that recognition.

To this end, what now follows is a short list of some of the bigger and more prominent blunders made by humanity through the last 2,000 years. In retrospect, it has become unquestionably clear to us from these examples that blunders have indeed been made, with likelihood of course of more to follow. Our culture, having once embarked upon an inappropriate idiosyncrasy, will as like as not be reluctant to let it go. Various factors may then keep it with us for a surprising amount of time. It may take *centuries* for the penny to finally drop and for replacement thinking to be accepted; and sadly, some problems resulting from much earlier times still remain with us to this day. There seems to be a marked tendency for people to become conditioned into a particular way of thinking such that there is a desire to cling to old concepts in order to preserve the status quo—often motivated by either a personal greed or by a fear of losing one's professional standing; and sometimes by individuals simply not wishing to drift away from their familiar flock. So let us begin with a brief account of the asbestos saga that is now widely acknowledged as having been a ghastly mistake responsible for the shortening of many lives:

1. <u>ASBESTOS AND ASBESTOSIS:</u> Asbestos has been long regarded as a useful mineral—from very early times. The Greek sculptor Callimachus used the fibres in 436 BC for the wick of the golden lamp in the temple of Pallas Athene. Romans of the 1st century mined the mineral for their textile

industry—making clothing, table cloths and napkins. The latter could be conveniently laundered by simply placing the items on the fire to burn off food stains, and its fire-resistance was also made use of in the wicks of 'eternal' lamps of the Vestal Virgins. But the historian Pliny, the elder, warned even at that early time of its toxicity, advising: *not to buy slaves from the asbestos mines because they will be ill and short-lived.* But despite this statement, business means money and the industry continued while sadly many died as the result. Leaping ahead to the time of our Industrial Revolution, rampant through the 18th century—many people at that time became factory workers. Some industries were healthy while others were not so. Asbestos-linked industries were clearly problematical, but quite often it was a decade or two of exposure before the disease symptoms of workers showed. By the late 19th century medical practitioners had linked asbestos to lung disease. In 1906 the first documented case of asbestos-linked disease was confirmed, the term 'asbestosis' emerging later. But the mining, the industrial usage and the deaths continued. As a part of World War II activity, shipyards became heavy users, it being used for insulation purpose. The yards were rushed with much ship-building and ship refits. Poor working conditions prevailed and placed more lives at risk resulting in many more early deaths. Through the latter 20th century, controls were only slowly put into place—import restrictions, workplace regulations and finally asbestos removal programs accompanied by air monitoring to safeguard those engaged in that irksome task. (As a scientific consultant at that time I was often called upon for analysis of insulation materials and to conduct air monitoring to accompany asbestos removal.) And so it took humanity almost 2,000 years following that first warning from Pliny, to clean up its act regarding this insidious industry. Even so, it is estimated that 5,000 tons went into the building of the World Trade Centre and much of this would have transferred to the New York atmosphere during the 9/11 event. So sadly, asbestos diseases and attendant lawsuits will continue almost certainly at least into the mid-21st century.

2. THE ROMAN CATHOLIC MISCONCEPTIONS: On the day of the death of Constantius Chlorus at York, UK; his son and fellow military campaigner Constantine was hailed by the troops as their new Augustus. Thus, here in the UK, began Constantine's rise to power that would lead to his uniting the Eastern and Western Roman Empires. The same Constantine arranged and presided over the Council of Nicaea in the year 325 that would launch into existence a Roman Catholic State-affiliated Religion that would subjugate much of the world. The new religion's central features of 'Trinity' and 'Creed' were devised by the young Deacon Athanasius, then still in his twenties. But he spoke well and the emperor was favourably impressed. But at that time, the most learned Arius of Alexandria had correctly taught that Jesus had been a man, who was in receipt of divine inspiration and was *not* co-equal with God. Despite Arius having many followers, Constantine rejected that teaching and had him excommunicated as heretic. The new Roman Catholic state religion united the two halves of Constantine's empire—East and West—and any dissenters were either exiled or executed. And so from its very beginning, this new religion with its new concepts ignored the

'love' teaching of Jesus and the 'thou shalt not kill' and 'love thy neighbour' Commandments given much earlier to Moses. It also ignored the fact that Athanasius was later removed from office on a number of charges and spent time hiding from authorities in a remote part of the Egyptian desert. But the religion gave Constantine's Empire strength and the Empire gave strength to the religion; albeit accompanied by continued killings and much feared torture policies. Ongoing periods of atrocity featured nine bloody crusades, the Papal Inquisition (1233), the Spanish Inquisition (1478 – 1834), the Roman Inquisition (1542 – 1700) and exterminations of Waldenses and Albigenses. The scientist Giordano Bruno was burned at the stake (1600) for correctly stating Earth to be a planet that rotates about the sun and the renowned Galileo was placed under house arrest during his latter days, while *his* discoveries were regarded as heresy. Victor Hugo's estimate for the total number of deaths was five million. That is likely to be an under-estimate, and there was also the ugly malpractice of burning those suspected of being witches. Witch-burning was widespread and ongoing. The last witch-suspect to be executed in UK was 1684 and in Poland 1792. The last UK arrest and imprisonment under the act was 19th January 1944, that of the wonderfully-developed medium Helen Duncan; with a final repeal of that act in 1951. There has also been associated lynching by mobs in Africa and in the Americas—continuing into the 20th century. So the Roman Catholic religion has a truly abysmal record of violence, murder, suppression and wrong thinking. It has been responsible for a doctrine of fear and has amassed for itself much wealth. And, as with our asbestos dalliance, it seems to be taking the best part of two millennia to resolve its grip on society.

During Salumet's visit of 4th April 2005, his words to us included:

~ **"Earthly religions will have their day when people realize that there is but one truth, one creator, one who loves and nurtures all things, all experiences, all planets, all universes, all of life. Yes, this religion** (Roman Catholic) **has limited time. The people within your world are now able to think and to feel and to see for themselves. This I gave to you previously when I told you that each successive generation will not take any form of religion at its face value."**

Later, 20th September 2010, Salumet elaborated:

~ **"I have listened to your words about decline in the papal religion—and, yes, some time past I told you that this would be so—but the reason I have come to you this time, is to say: there is much unrest in all forms of religion. At last, your young people are beginning to think for themselves. No longer will they accept the blind faith of their parents and elders. The time is coming for** *all* **religions to look at themselves honestly and squarely—the first steps have already been taken. For this, my dear friends, I would say to you—rejoice! Because at last, the truth of all 'love and existence' will belong to all people— no longer will people just accept, blindly."**

These *facts* may rest uncomfortably with some, but they are indeed substantiated *facts* from which each of us is free to draw our own conclusions.

3. CIGARETTES, TOBACCO AND CANCER: Native Americans would pass and share the peace pipe charged with tobacco or red willow bark—the thought being that the little puff of smoke would carry their prayers to Heaven. And Aztec and Maya smoked as part of *their* spiritual ceremonies. These early beginnings are a far cry from the excesses of the Western world—the huge and highly toxic industry that the Western world has made of tobacco; the tobacco first being impregnated with various chemicals, then marketed and smoked to excess purely for pleasure, with no spiritual connection. (I will not list the 599 permitted chemical additives that are not required to be listed on the packet!) The improved mechanisation for cigarette manufacture towards the end of the 19th century was to lead to much more widespread smoking popularity and to a serious worldwide epidemic of lung cancer. The smoking cult has been further encouraged by the billions spent on really heavy advertising, film star posturing and free issue 'smokes' to UK, US and Russian military. Today's lead country for manufacture is China, followed by Russia and US. China currently makes 2.4 trillion cigarettes annually—40 % of the almost 6 trillion world annual output. Our planet now has in excess of 500 cigarette factories and the modern PROTOS-M8 manufacturing machine can turn out 9 million cigarettes in one single 8-hour shift. Nicotine, tobacco's active principle is addictive and the cigarette is now seen as *the biggest cause of preventable death*

in the world. Recent annual death figures indicate 443,000 in US and almost 6 million worldwide. Of the 4,000 chemicals identified in cigarette smoke, at least 73 are known carcinogens. The link to lung cancer has been known to the Western world from around 1940, but the evidence for it has been vigorously challenged by those wishing to keep the highly profitable industry in operation. Many of course continue smoking as the result of addiction. There is also the added complication of large tax revenues that have been a further impediment to abolition. A little progress towards moderation has been achieved however, with some countries outlawing cigarette advertisement, banning smoking in hospitals and a number of public places, raising additional tax on the product and by spreading awareness of the risks involved. But this very serious man-made health problem continues still, on a huge worldwide scale, while in addition, even the old cigarette butts have become a garbage problem on certain otherwise beautiful beaches. So the problems from this horrendous highly toxic blunder are as I write still very much with us.

4. NUCLEAR MISSILE THREAT: We shall be describing in the next chapter how Dmitri Mendeleev became aware of the Periodic Classification of chemical elements. It is a natural phenomenon that elements comprising the larger more complex atoms of that periodic classification have a measure of instability that has become known as 'radioactive decay'. The French chemist Henri Bequerel discovered (1896) that uranium salts emit something that passes through protective film to blacken a photographic plate, as does light without any

protection. So why is this?—and what exactly is radioactive decay? It is in essence the ejection of energy and particles from a proportion of the atomic nucleus. The rate at which this happens is measured in terms of elemental 'half-life'—the time taken for half the atoms to decay. The dangers from exposure were not at first realised, so that early researchers doing valuable work, suffered radiation burns, hair loss and sickness. Marie Curie died of aplastic anaemia, most probably due to her working environment. Even so, some physicians and corporations most unwisely and incautiously made the decision to market medicinal tonics and treatments based on radioactive salts—a radium enema included! Marie Curie had raised her objection to this but to no avail and deaths resulted, and so the term 'radioactive quackery' was coined. By the 1930s such products had been removed from the market. There have been more rational applications of radioactive salts; for example, as tracers, leak detectors and as a means of archaeological dating. But perhaps the major development has been electric power generation. There are both advantages and disadvantages where this use is concerned. The process is fairly clean in as much as the atmosphere is little fouled, but there is a difficult nuclear waste disposal problem, decommissioning of plant is both lengthy and costly and there have been accidents—Chernobyl, Ukraine and Fukushima, Japan being extremely serious examples. There are without doubt methods of power generation that are cleaner, much safer and less harmful to our planet. But by far the biggest problem has been, and still is, the irrational emphasis on military applications.

The destruction of two Japanese cities at the conclusion of World War II amply illustrates the destructive potential of nuclear bombs and missiles. Huge incautious stock-piling of nuclear weapons, their further development and upgraded delivery systems has since followed, utilising massive funds that could have been spent in a constructive way instead of placing planetary population under threat of annihilation. So in terms of wasted funds, fear-induction, accident risk with its damage to environment, nuclear missiles must be seen as a fourth huge blunder that now urgently requires correction.

Having referenced four unquestionably major blunders made by mankind—almost entirely attributable to *man*-kind as opposed to *woman*-kind—let us now turn our attention to very recent and therefore a little less obvious major *scientific* blunders, each in some measure connected and each still the subject of quite vigorous debate:

5. MODERN SCIENCE, MATERIALISM AND BIG BANG: First of all, there has been the failure of scientific mainstream to take seriously our *spirit connection*. Secondly, there has been more than a century of *aether denial*. Thirdly, our science has dwelt on the erroneous *big bang theory* that despite its various modifications, fails to convincingly explain cosmology.

6. SPIRIT: The Society for Psychical Research was founded in London, UK (1882), with its stated objectives: to understand events and abilities ascribed to psychic and paranormal phenomena. And then, formation of the American

Society for Psychical Research quickly followed (1884). These were worthy first moves, but from the very outset there were two camps in the community at large—those who were true seekers and those bent on exposing fraud. The exposure of silly self-centred fraudsters, of course satisfied mainstream sceptics. Fraudsters have been such a bothersome nuisance to the societies and they deserve strong condemnation. And the two camps of researchers have been mirrored by two camps within the wider public domain. Within the public domain there are those that as the result of first-hand experience, *know* truth; and there are opinionated sceptical materialists who simply *do not* know. Mainstream science and its peer-reviewed journals have so far favoured the latter stance; concentrating mainly on physical matters whilst showing very little interest in truly spiritual concepts and happenings. But there are signs of change within this overall picture.

7. <u>AETHER</u>: Following initial interpretation of the Michelson-Morley experiment of 1887, aether existence has been denied by scientific majority in the West—there has been just so much credence placed in that initial finding. The experiments were conducted with the utmost care but doubt has since been cast on interpretation of the results. How this came about is accounted in some detail in chapter 4 and so will not be repeated here. This highly significant part of the creation process continues to be disregarded by scientific majority. Eventually, aether-existence must again be acknowledged, and this will doubtless lead to a realistic understanding of gravity; also to a much improved understanding of cosmology in general.

8. <u>BIG BANG THEORY:</u> This was the brainchild of Belgian physicist Georges Lemaître. He had published a paper in 1927 detailing solutions to Einstein's General Relativity equations for an expanding universe—this in itself no small achievement. But the exercise had later led to the notion of *universe expansion from a point source at some specific moment in time* and so this possibility was explored. Edwin Hubble, using the large telescope on Mount Wilson, California, had noted that the further galaxies were moving away faster than those closer to us—at speeds roughly proportional to their distances. The universe was seen to be expanding from every point (as does baker's dough) and Hubble had noted the movements. The relatively new 100-inch Hooker telescope on Mount Wilson was at that time the world's largest, its 2-ton fused glass lens-blank having been allowed more than one full year to cool to avoid cracking! The telescope had in itself been a most worthy project! And so, with Hubble's supporting observations of the heavens to back up Lemaître's concept, the Big Bang theory was born; it being calculated that the universe must have suddenly come into existence 13,700 billion years ago as one hot exploding point source. And as further supporting evidence, an existing cosmic microwave background was thought to be residual heat from that very first 'big bang' explosion. But all is not explained and huge problems remain. Attendant to the concept of Big Bang, it is necessary to make the assumption that 73% of the universe consists of a mysterious 'dark energy', while a further 23% consists of an equally mysterious 'dark matter'—only 4.6% being physical matter as we know it and as we are able to observe it. So we must accept straight away that the

Big Bang theory is much troubled with major problems and work on these problems continues. On the face of it, the Big Bang accounts a very minor fraction of the universe and we are expected to take on trust 96% that is unseen and undefined, calling it *dark energy* and *dark matter* and still with no mention of any part being played by an all-pervading *aether*. It must also be pointed out that our astronomers are permitted to observe only a tiny fraction of the total cosmos— a fraction of unknown size; or if infinite, then that is something that we would fail to understand anyway. Perhaps therefore to attempt accounting for the entire creation in this way is stepping off limits from what one might consider to be rational possibility. But such is the process of inquiry that engages the human intellect, and the intellect can so easily get stuck on a wayward theme and it can, as we have seen in retrospect, make blunders.

CHAPTER 3 - PIONEERS OF THE MORE RECENT PROGRESS

Much of the progress made by our scientists has of course been excellent. Truly majestic progress was made through our 17th century and onwards. A number of names are much revered and rightly so. Chemical elements and units of measure have been named after them, and so, their memory will live on in scientific and sometimes in public domain.

Isaac Newton (1642 – 1727): Rumour has it that it was a falling apple that first inspired this gentleman and led to publication of his *Principia* in 1687—a great work setting out the laws of motion and gravitation within this universe. If gravity draws an apple from a tree, then it must also reach to the moon and hold our *Queen of the Night* in orbit. That would properly explain the nature of orbit and similar motions in this universe! He was able to describe in wonderfully elegant terms all observed universal motions, but not its prime cause—not the modus operandi of gravitational acceleration. That would have to wait. Some were unhappy at having to accept the principle of *action at a distance* with no apparent reason given. Galileo Galilei (1564 – 1642) had already demonstrated that balls of differing mass when dropped from a tower fall with exactly the same acceleration, each striking the ground at exactly the same time. Perhaps there is a clue here. Experiments would later demonstrate that without air friction—as in a vacuum—lead shot and a feather also fall with the same acceleration. So while Newton's work was a stupendous step forward for humanity, one had in his day to simply accept gravity as a mysterious *action at a distance* fact, with no understanding at all of its mechanism. But Newton's laws of motion are accurately stated, his 3rd law being: 'Action and reaction are always equal and opposite'. We had on 16th November 2009 placed a question to our guide Salumet about space rockets and his reply included:

~ **"I would only say that every action has some reaction. That applies whether you are here on Earth or on another planet or in space. There is always an effect for any action."**

So quite by chance we have actually received confirmation from spirit of Newton's 3rd law!

Gotfried Leibniz (1646 – 1716): This contemporary of Newton, living in Germany was also an inspired one. It might be said that his 'Monadology' (1714) was a mechanical forerunner to our much later notion of quantized space—in modern quantum mechanics a quantum is considered to be one discrete unit of energy that cannot be subdivided, and some have considered so-called 'aether-space' to be quantized. Leibniz had stated:

"Now where there are no parts, there neither extension, nor shape, nor divisibility is possible. And these monads are the true atoms of nature..."

True atoms/units of nature indeed, and the basis of everything! Leibniz and Newton also it seems, both invented and used the mathematical system 'Differential Calculus' each calling it by different names. Leibniz invented the 'binary code', 0110110, that is the basis of our computer language today, and he invented our world's first 'calculator' to be mass produced—so this one and Newton were admirable thinkers to herald this present time of more rapid growth.

Christiaan Huygens (1629 – 1695): This Dutch gentleman knew Baruch Spinoza and Antoni van Leeuwenhoek—both expert lens grinders. The latter built surprisingly good microscopes. But Huygens was more interested in the telescope, and by studying the rings of Saturn he discovered its moon 'Titan'. But it is for his realizing and describing the wave-character of light that he is to be especially remembered. A contemporary, René Descartes (remembered for Cartesian co-ordinates—the x/y axes in graph presentation) had predicted future greatness for Huygens. Sadly, that greatness came *well into the future*, it being another150-years or so before his wave theory of light would be fully accepted by the world! It sometimes takes time and the world has to wait, but others followed with their observations and experiments that would prove his theory entirely correct—so, just as sound waves are known to travel through air, light-waves likewise travel through something as a waveform, and that something would be the aether.

Ole Rømer (1644 – 1710): If light travels through the aether as a waveform, then it must have a velocity and that velocity must be measurable. This Danish astronomer made a meticulous study of the moons of Jupiter. The moon 'Io' and the planet's other moons rotate with uniform motion, as does Earth's moon. In drawing up a timetable for their passage, he noticed one odd discrepancy—when Jupiter was further away from Earth, *its moons got behind schedule*; but in the season when Jupiter came closer to Earth *its moons were ahead of schedule*! He reasoned from this that light must have finite velocity and the observed differences in its moon-rotation times could only be due to the extra distance that light travels in its journey to Earth. So this astronomer became the first to provide a measurement for *speed of light*, thus providing support for Huygens' travelling wave theory.

Armand Fizeau (1819 – 1896): We are indebted to this French physicist for devising an apparatus capable of more accurate measurement of light velocity. He found a way of timing light along a 16-kilometre path. His apparatus included a *rapidly* rotating toothed wheel and a mirror positioned 8-kilometres away. A light beam passed between wheel-teeth to be reflected by the mirror and return through an adjacent wheel-tooth. This well-thought-out arrangement gave a value of 313,000,000 metres/sec, [the value considered correct today lies very close to 300, 000,000 metres/sec]. So Huygens had very clearly been correct with his wave theory—Fizeau's result and the way it was obtained left no room for any possible doubt! And he was also able to predict the 'red shift' of light received from a receding distant source—this phenomenon and significance of it to be mentioned later.

James Clerk Maxwell (1831 – 1879): At quite an early age this Scottish mathematician and physicist demonstrated with spinning tops that the colours red, green and blue in combination, made white. Now that is interesting—a sunlight spectrum illustrated in reverse? But his huge contribution to our way forward was a set of equations. These describe electromagnetism in mathematical terms and show how electric and magnetic fields relate to each other. His equations involve what are known as Faraday's law, Ampère's law, Lenz's law and Gauss's law. [These laws are complex and describe induction by a changing magnetic field, how magnetic field relates to electric current, EM circuits and Newton's 3rd law (of action and reaction), and to the charge distribution in a field.] And a light wave could be described as 'polarized' with both electric and magnetic fields perpendicular to direction of travel and to each other (there is an oscillating electric field and an oscillating magnetic field that are perpendicular to each other; also perpendicular to the direction of travel of the light-wave). While *natural light* carries its oscillations in all directions, there are ways of restricting that polarization to one single direction—passage through the mineral feldspar for example can achieve this. Today, we are using this principle of course, when using Polaroid sun glasses to reduce brightness without any further thought; but such things are the result of a great deal of study by those clever thinkers of earlier times.

<u>Heinrich Hertz (1857 – 1894)</u>: The work of Maxwell might well be described as brilliantly theoretical and accurately predictive. That work concerned light, plus *possibly* other EM waves. It became the far-sighted aim of this German physicist to reduce all physical phenomena to the discipline of 'mechanics'. He succeeded in building an apparatus that would produce and receive radio waves. He was able to confirm that the longer, non-visible EM waves of Maxwell's conception do indeed exist and they do indeed compare with light waves—comparing in regard to such properties as their velocity, reflectance, refraction, interference and they can be polarized. It follows that the various EM waves, whether visible or not, are all 'aether undulations' as is sunlight. He was furthermore able to demonstrate how certain materials transmit these EM waves while others reflect (and this would eventually lead to the development of radar). Tragically, this brilliant and acclaimed scientist died of a medical condition at the tender age of 36, but he achieved so much in a short life, and it is appropriate that the 'hertz' unit of frequency should be so named in his honour.

<u>Michael Faraday (1791 – 1867)</u>: So we now know that the same velocity is shared by all those electromagnetic waves that ride on the aether medium. Therefore, it is the nature of the medium that determines EM-velocity and not wavelength of the travelling undulation. This English scientist would now add much more to our understanding of electromagnetism and of electromagnetic effects. As third child of four in a family that was not at all well off, he received only a meagre education; being largely self-taught, but with such a strong

drive and a powerful curiosity, that did not seem to matter—he worked hard, impressed contacts to become an accomplished scientist of his day. He explored the magnetic field around an electric current, discovering the laws of electromagnetic induction, diamagnetism and electrolysis. He discovered that the plane of polarized light can be rotated by an applied magnetic field and he showed that magnetism can affect light in a dielectric material such as glass. His inventions include a dynamo—ancestor of modern power generators. He is hailed as one of the greatest of scientists but he was highly principled and did not seek wealth or aggrandisement; refusing a knighthood and presidency of the Royal Society. And when asked by government if he would advise on the production of chemical weapons to be used in the Crimean war, he was sufficiently rational to refuse that assignment on ethical grounds. So he was a truly great scientist and with principles to boot; and we know that Albert Einstein kept three pictures side by side on his study wall: Isaac Newton, James Clerk Maxwell and Michael Faraday.

So following the endeavours of these notaries of science, and of course the endeavours of many others, we perhaps begin to understand just a little more about how the mysteries leading up to present times have been unravelled; also how their work connects via light's intriguing properties to the aether—that mysterious fifth element. It not only carries the light waves but a huge range of waves that we may now collectively describe as 'electromagnetic' on account of their transverse electric and magnetic oscillations. There now remains no doubt whatsoever that these EM waves exist, and in our modern world we have learned to make use of many frequencies; notably radio, TV, computer programs, email communication and mobile phones. And how nice it is that so many nations have been involved in these developments! But scientific language continues to evolve and the word 'element' has now of course taken on new meaning. In today's terminology the aether is a medium—a medium that conducts EM waves. 'Elements' have become chemical entities comprised of units called atoms and molecules. It is therefore appropriate that at this stage we cite the work of one further scientist, a little ahead of schedule perhaps—a chemist—who did so much to clarify the nature and arrangement of elements:

Dmitri Mendeleef (1834 – 1907): Born in a Siberian village near Tobolsk, his mother managed to make the journey with him across Russia and to St Petersburg where he was able to study chemistry. A big thank you to his mum for completing that mammoth journey! Now here we introduce a little chemical data: The number of discovered chemical elements had been steadily growing and when Mendeleef published his work on them there were just sixty (119 listed today), and their atomic weights had been determined—atomic weight being mass of one single atom compared to hydrogen, the lightest and simplest element. But sixty was enough for him to realize that when they were placed in order of atomic weight and valence (the bonding ratio with other elements) a periodicity became apparent. So he drew up what he called a 'Periodic Table' to show this. (It is now known that the periodicity is due to the number of electrons in the outer shell of each atom, which fact also determines valence grouping in the table). I understand that the table, virtually as published, finally came to him in a dream and he was quick to write it down on waking! It was a big step forward for science.

> *"It is the function of science to discover the existence of a general reign of order in nature and to find the causes governing this order."*
>
> *Dmitri Mendeleef.*

Mendeleef had noticed that there were several gaps in his table of sixty elements. He surmised that these would be filled by elements yet to be discovered, and he gave their approximate atomic weights. He was correct!

In order to keep the data fairly simple I will list only the first two short periods of elements in what is still called the Periodic Table:

Group:	1.	2.	3.	4.	5.	6.	7.	8.
1st Period	Li	Be	B	C	N	O	F	Ne
2nd Period	Na	Mg	Al	Si	P	S	Cl	Ar

[The symbols are: Li = lithium, Be = beryllium, B = boron, C = carbon, N = nitrogen, O = oxygen, F = fluorine, Ne = neon, Na = sodium (natrium), Mg = magnesium, Al = aluminium, Si = silicon, P = phosphorus, S = sulphur, Cl = chlorine, Ar = argon.

[And a rather bright lecturer once said to his class: Think of the (fictitious) Russian chemist 'Libebcnofne' and his wife 'Namgalsipsclar' and you have the first two periods committed to memory—and so, sixty years on I am still able to write down the above sequence just like that!].

Group numbers relate to valence and we now know that these numbers represent the number of electrons in the outer atom. We also know that a set of eight electrons fills the outer shell of the atom and confers stability. Common salt may be written as its formula NaCl—the one electron of sodium joining with the seven electrons of chlorine to make a stable octet of electrons, hence NaCl is a stable molecule of salt—that is how the chemistry works. The 'group 8' elements already possess a stable octet of electrons and are therefore very, very reluctant to form any compounds. But I now would like to point out some of the special qualities of the group 4 element: carbon. This element has a number of allotropic forms (carbon atoms can link together in several different ways) including the well-known 'graphite'—its atoms are arranged in sheets, making it opaque to light and slippery (a graphite pencil will glide easily across a piece of paper leaving a trail). Diamond is a very different allotrope of carbon, its hard 3-dimensional lattice structure *allowing light to pass through,* albeit much more slowly than its passage through the aether. But what makes the element carbon *really* special is the way it can form literally millions of compounds by combining with itself, with hydrogen, oxygen, nitrogen, sulphur and with many other elements. Many of the compounds include *chains* of carbon atoms and some *6-atom ring* structures—and quite literally they all form part of life's rich pattern! Silicon, being adjacent to carbon in group 4, also does this, but only to a limited extent. But by virtue of its complex nature carbon is *the element of life* here on Earth—all life. It is the element that makes all our planetary lives here on Earth possible. Now that is one profound chemical statement! We had inquired of our knowledgeable extraterrestrial friend Bonniol if it is the same on his planet. He had hesitated in his reply, explaining that the chemistry was a little different on his planet on account of its elements having higher vibrations. This made it difficult for him—a physical being—to give a clear-cut answer. BUT knowledgeable ones in spirit had been watching over the exchange and a messenger was sent through to provide a clear answer for us:

~ *"I am here to say one thing. I'm sent to tell you: Your discussion about CARBON—yes, I am instructed to tell you: IT IS A FUNDAMENTAL ELEMENT OF ALL THE UNIVERSE. And it will exist on the planet you have been speaking about, although as they have told you, at a different rate of vibration. But in all the cosmos, this exists because it is a 'regenerative force' on all LIVING planets. The only time it (the situation) changes is in spirit. So that point has to be made, and that is why I am here."*

How very nice to have that confirmation! And our visitor was very warmly thanked. So the element carbon has indeed its place throughout this universe where planetary life is concerned, and the meaning of 'regenerative' here is: as viewed from spirit, life can be 'regenerated from spirit' on a suitably evolved planet that has the element carbon. And it now goes without saying that 'suitably evolved' includes an amazing degree of order. During our meeting of 11th May 2009, I spoke with Salumet about the orderliness scientists were finding, actually naming a short list of elements; also commenting on the orderliness of EM-wave frequencies. I inquired if it was likewise in spirit. His reply:

~ **"Let me first say to you that all of creation is 'orderly' as you say. Without it there would be chaos—I believe that is one of the words that you use** (agreed). **Your scientists— your physicists—all of your 'ists' in your world are looking and searching for more knowledge. That is the nature of humankind. That is part of being human, and yes, there has to be order within spirit. Your scientists will continue to discover more and more, but infinite knowledge will never be made known to them, because of the very fact of being human, but there is still much that they can discover about spirit and the continuance of the life force."**

Well, perhaps those two statements received from spirit sum up the ground covered thus far rather better than I could have managed. So up to and well into the 19th century humankind had been making useful headway in the gathering together of knowledge whilst at the same time the aether continued to be acknowledged by scientific majority. And today, some of us are able to discuss Earthly progress with those in spirit, embellish facts and make just a little more sense of it all.

Finally, as a fitting tribute to the work of Dmitri Mendeleef, element 101 of the Periodic Table has been named 'Mendelevium'.

CHAPTER 4 – THE MICHELSON-MORLEY
EXPERIMENT AND ITS AFTERMATH

It is clear that the scientists named in chapter 3 and their colleagues had successfully continued to seek further understanding and they had also continued to acknowledge existence of the aether medium. But as our planet orbits the sun, travelling at about 30 Km/sec it was felt that it should be possible to detect its passage *through* the aether by demonstrating the presence of an 'aether wind'. And so, two physicists in the US, Albert Michelson and Edward Morley were commissioned to set about this task. They built an 'interferometer' apparatus that by means of silvered and half-silvered mirrors would split a light beam in two, sending out each half on paths perpendicular to one another in a horizontal plane, to then be re-combined, forming interference fringes that could be examined. A fringe displacement as a result of this was expected. But there was some difficulty in devising an apparatus of sufficient sensitivity and a 100% positive result was not obtained. This was in the year 1887. The attempted detection of an aether wind using refined equipment was repeated by Michelson and Morley; also by several others. Discussions that followed became complex, referring to 'sensitivity of equipment', 'calculated limits of error', 'components of sidereal aether drift', 'favoured

45

experiment locations' and 'possible relativistic effects'. The end result of a huge amount of honest endeavour was that *mainstream science considered aether to be a myth*— unrevealed by experiment and unnecessary for light passage. After all, the set of four equations of James Clerk Maxwell describe light as an electromagnetic wave-form and this was seen as sufficient description in itself. Light appeared to be *a law unto itself* with no dependence upon any medium for its transit across the universe. That was to become the conclusion.

It was a turning point and a sad day for mainstream science when aether's existence came to be denied, and that sad day extended to become one sad century—so scientists made the mistake of denying aether existence throughout the entire 20th century. A number of leading scientists also denied or gave no thought to the 'spiritual existence', so that the accepted thought pattern became very much a materialistic one. On reflection, it can now be seen that scientific development had its wayward and unacceptable side right through that period— weaponry, explosives, toxic gases for two world wars, defoliating and deforming Agent Orange, devastating nuclear missiles, their testing and their delivery systems—even high-altitude megaton detonations (Project Starfish 1962) disturbing Earth's protective Van Allen radiation belt! Sir Martin Ryle, Britain's Astronomer Royal had filed formal objection to that particular project but his input had been ignored. In the following year the US, Soviet Union and UK were signatories to a Limited Test Ban Treaty for nuclear weapons, allowing in future only underground testing. That put a stop to the high-altitude disruptions and to atmospheric pollutions at least. Other questionable developments included the highly toxic so-called pesticides and internal combustion engines that, as deployed and used, resulted in more atmospheric pollution—all these things leading to serious upset of nature's delicate balance. Change was desperately needed. Happily, not all scientists were caught up in this problematic and irresponsible treadmill—there was also useful progress. But of course, the institutions, the universities, most publishers and elected governments all aligned to the mainstream development; so the voices of those *not* caught up in retrograde activities tended not to be heard. But thankfully for us all, there were indeed other voices.

Albert Einstein (1879 – 1955): The voice of this philosophical physicist has of course left us with a huge legacy of intelligent thought to peruse. During childhood, his father had shown him a magnetic compass. So something invisible must be responsible for moving the needle! And this led to an early essay when he was but a 16-year-old: 'On the Nature of the State of the Aether in a Magnetic Field'. His essay concerned electric current and how its magnetic field might in reality be a deformed elastic aether—an interesting thought from a mere 16-year-old! But his first authoritative pillar of 20th century science was introduced in 1905 with *'Special Relativity'* which united Maxwell's laws with mechanics, the latter requiring some modification near the speed of light. And then Special Relativity, which few in this world could understand at the time, was quickly followed by his mass-energy equivalence equation which is perhaps more readily comprehensible:

$$E = mc^2$$

So in the final analysis, *all* the material world is energy (E), equivalent to the right hand side of the above equation (mass times speed-of-light squared)—equally of course, spirit world is also entirely energy from which the aether and then our material world have been created. Einstein's '*General Relativity*' followed in 1915 in which 'gravity' is described as the warping of a 4-dimensional space-time (3-dimensions of space plus time, seen as a 4th dimension)—pictured for the sake of simplicity as a flat 2-dimensional grid. Anything heavy such as a planet resting on the grid would then depress it as if it were a rubber sheet—the 2-dimensional grid being purely a clever device for getting our minds around the idea of four dimensions that could be warped. Planetary spin would also exert a twisting influence on that grid. [But perhaps we should not overlook the possibility that distortions of our imagined grid are in reality some kind of manipulation of the aether].

So, Einstein's statement of mass-energy equivalence equates our material world *entirely* to energy, and he does not stand alone in that affirmation. During our evening of 10th November 1997, Salumet was asked about the demise of trees that do not last forever as trees. In his reply our guide spoke of the ongoing energy of the tree, that still continues:

~"**After all, if you take your planet, it is just one mass of energy that belongs to the wider scheme of the Universe, so each living thing within this planet, belongs to the larger whole. Plant energy would in effect return, when it is decayed, to the soil, which is also energy. It is a continuing process, which can never be destroyed.**"

More was said on 22nd October 2001. I had placed a question relating to 'dimensions' here on Earth and in spirit to which Salumet responded:

~"**I think that first we must define the word dimension, if you are to understand what I am saying to you. What is dimension? It is nothing but a transmutation of energy. Do you understand? All is energy, all these dimensions you speak of, are but a transmutation of the same energy. When you speak of a level that I come from, then all of this energy would become part of—There is no what you call, 'dimension.' We are in a difficult subject here my friends...**"

Difficult indeed!—but the point is well made that *all is energy*. And another—an inspired one from our 20th century had an intriguing way of putting it:

49

*"The tendency of modern physics is to resolve the whole
material universe into waves and nothing but waves; these are
waves of two kinds; bottled up waves which we call matter
and un-bottled waves which we call radiation or light. If
annihilation of matter occurs, the process is merely that of un-
bottling imprisoned wave energy and letting it fall to travel
through space. These concepts reduce the whole universe to a
world of light, potential and existence, so that the whole story
of creation can be told with perfect accuracy and
completeness in the six words, "God said, 'Let there be
light'."*

Sir James Jeans, The Mysterious Universe, (1930).

So, the aether and EM waveform carried by that aether has to
be acknowledged as a vital step in an ongoing creation
process, and in the final analysis of that ongoing creation
process *all* is energy. Every atom and each particle within the
atom—each electron—all is some form of energy. We have
already mentioned the part played by electrons when atoms
link together to form the substances of nature, and these
minute negatively charged particles have been the object of
further informative study. It has been possible to accelerate
electrons to very *nearly* the speed of light (c). But on nearing
c, much more energy must be applied to produce more speed.
That the mass of the electron increases and approaches
infinity, has been put forward as an explanation for this
phenomenon; but why should this be? And an applied
magnetic field to pull the travelling particles off course would
appear to confirm such explanation, there being little effect as
the velocity c is approached. These were admirable, carefully
conducted experiments and understandable thought
constructions, much more easily said than done! BUT all this
transpired in the 20th century when existence of the aether was
rigorously denied by all those boffins, which made a more

50

satisfactory explanation of results extremely difficult or virtually impossible. A magical mass increase to infinity with no explanation as to why is hardly satisfactory! Acceptance of aether and explanation in terms of the build-up of some form of aether 'bow wave' on nearing c would seem rather more plausible. Furthermore, this would compare most favourably with the aeronautics phenomenon of 'sound barrier' resulting in a 'sonic boom' as an aircraft approaches the speed of sound in air. So perhaps we should consider these elegant and most carefully conducted experiments with accelerated electrons as a proof of aether's existence!

Following the honest endeavours and findings of Maxwell, Michelson, Morley and Einstein, there has been much spurious talk and theorizing about 'empty space', but space of course in reality, cannot by any stretch of the imagination be considered as empty. Concerning the implications of the work of Einstein one can really do no better than to consider how *he himself* has reviewed his own work a few years following those intriguing relativity publications. On 5th May 1920 he gave an address at the University of Leiden entitled 'Aether and the Theory of Relativity'. In that address, some perfectly clear statements were made:

"...the special theory of relativity does not compel us to deny aether. We may assume the existence of an aether, only we must give up ascribing a definite state of motion to it..."

He goes on to elaborate the idea of our 4-dimensional world as being composed of world-threads of particulate matter, then continuing:

"The special theory of relativity forbids us to assume the aether to consist of particles observable through time, but the

51

hypothesis of aether in itself is not in conflict with the special theory of relativity. Only we must be on our guard against ascribing a state of motion to the aether."

But then we might ask ourselves the questions:

(1) How would we detect motion in aether in a lightless condition?
(2) How could aether be shaped into a light wave in the complete absence of any form of motion?

But then Einstein continued with a reference to his *general* theory:

"...we may say that according to the general theory of relativity space is endowed with physical qualities; in this sense, therefore, there exists an aether. According to the general theory of relativity space without aether is unthinkable; for in such space there would not only be no propagation of light, but also no possibility of existence for standards of space and time (measuring rods and clocks) nor therefore any space-time intervals..."

So this much revered gentleman's views on the aether are unequivocally stated by Einstein himself. He is clearly, or was at that time, of the opinion that aether exists—but perhaps we should consider or re-consider carefully what he had to say about the motion of it. This will become clearer later. And we certainly cannot of course view aether movement as a stream of moving particles—the medium being non-particulate. But perhaps there is motion or modification within it that we would not normally assign to or attribute to in the material way of thinking. So perhaps we should *be on our guard* concerning aether's motion, but that is not to say that motion in some guise must be ruled out.

Since Einstein's publications there has been some validation of his relativity theory—the theory had predicted several cosmological qualities that have since been observed. These include:
Gravitational lensing: Light rays are bent by massive objects in the heavens; this to such an extent as to make it possible for astronomers to see around massive objects at great distance.

Dragging of space-time by planetary rotation: Axes of gyroscopes carried by the satellite 'Gravity Probe B' launched by NASA (2004) were seen to drift slightly in compliance with that part of Einstein's theory.

Gravitational red shift (gravity influencing the frequency of EM-radiation): Two physicists, Robert Pound and Glen Rebka, sent gamma rays up a tower (1959) and the gamma ray frequency was observed to be very slightly shortened.
It might be said that these three items indicate that massive bodies in the universe exert their gravitational influence locally upon the aether.

Neither Maxwell's equations nor Einstein's relativity theory; or Einstein's mass-energy equivalence, actually include any symbol to denote aether; so viewed together with a negative Michelson-Morley interpretation, many have taken the view that space is simply empty—void of anything that might bestow observable properties. But this has left gravity and the effects of it unexplained, and has left light as an unexplained law unto itself, independent of any carrier. Furthermore, the equations *do include* expressions for 'space-time curvature', 'Newton's gravitational constant', Einstein's 'cosmological constant' (a value for energy density of space) and 'c'. So quite clearly, properties that should be pertaining to aether *are* involved in these equations. How might we set about creating a curve in nothing? How could we set about measuring a density value for nothing? Perhaps we should also observe that whilst Maxwell's equations brilliantly describe the electromagnetic nature of the travelling light wave—the wave's alternating electric and magnetic vectors—this of course does not exclude the possibility of it in addition being a compression wave. Alternate compression and rarefaction might even be instrumental in the generation of Maxwell's vectors. Even if the travelling light wave is torsional (of alternating twist character) neither does this rule out attendant compression and rarefaction. In any event it would be useful for us to know how 'electric' and 'magnetic' are generated from the 'non-material' source. And I feel sure we can all readily accept that 'electric' and 'magnetic' cannot be generated from nothing. We are dealing with a subject that is off-limits from the material world, so that different laws will prevail. We therefore have to proceed forward with due caution and with open minds—gaping wide-open minds!

PART 2 – UNIVERSAL LAWS AND THEORIES

CHAPTER 5 - LIGHT WAVE AND SOUND WAVE COMPARISONS

I t will be quickly noted that from making these wave comparisons, a strong case is made for the possibility that light, in addition to its long accepted electromagnetic character, is as in the case of sound, a compression wave. And in a compression wave, something has to be compressed. In making such a comparison, we must of course observe at the outset that sound concerns our familiar material world—is part of it, and it results from the jostling together of particulate matter—while light in itself involves no material substance. Light is not a compression of particulate bits and pieces. Sound is of a physical nature and is therefore confined to our planet where it can travel through air, through water and through various solid materials. It has a simple, easily understood direction of travel in air and in water, while the travel mode is just a little more complex through solids. An earthquake is a good example of wave travel in a solid, where the main wave/quake is followed by waves that are perpendicular to that main direction of motion. These perpendicular waves are called 'aftershocks'. So, the sound wave in rigid solids is that little bit different from its simpler nature in air and water; but all such waves are strictly confined to our planet—to our material world. We might even observe that for sound-in-a-solid and light-in-aether, each has a surprising component or components perpendicular to direction of travel. But of course, the light wave is very different from sound in that it can travel the entire universe through what has in the past been termed the 'luminiferous aether'. That latter term is now very much out of favour. In fact, I find that these days both luminiferous and aether get underlined in red by my computer program as if their use is improper; and in a dictionary, 'luminiferous' is either described as *archaic* or does not appear at all! And to describe aether as 'luminiferous', would of course credit it with light-carrying potential. While light and sound have the very basic differences described, it is nevertheless appropriate that we evaluate and compare the properties of each waveform because, as will become evident, they share key data concerning their mode of travel. And comparison of this key data should help us towards a much-improved understanding of environment generally. So let us begin by considering the nature of their velocities:

Velocity: Sound is regarded as a known compression wave that travels at fixed velocity through a specified medium and its details are fairly well understood. In general, it travels fastest in rigid solids (that have short distance between their ions), more slowly in solids that have more widely spaced ions, more slowly again in water and other liquids and slower still in air and various gases. So overall, the greater the distance between ions/molecules, the more slowly does the sound wave travel. A few examples that illustrate these facts are:

Table 1

Sound Velocities for a Range of Materials in Metres per Second (m/sec.):

Solids:	Velocity	Liquids:	Velocity	Gases:	Velocity
Diamond	12,000	Glycol	1,660	Hydrogen	1,290
Iron	5,130	Sea water	1,533	Helium	972
Copper	4,600	Water	1,493	Air	343
Glass	3,962	Alcohol	1,144	Oxygen	316
Lead	1,158	Ether	985	Ether (40^0C)	187

It will be seen that in solids, *rigidity plus low density* of the medium generally favours higher sound velocity. Short distances between ions/molecules and structural character contribute to rigidity. In general, sound is faster in solids than in liquids or gases. It is significant of course that in the latter, the molecules are spaced very much further apart.

As we know, light travels many times faster than sound. The value for light travelling in aether lies very close to 300,000,000 m/sec., the precise value measured being 299,792,458 m/sec. It always travels more slowly than this in transparent particulate materials—the higher the refractive index, the slower the light speed. So there would appear to be a slowing down due possibly to interaction between aether and ions/molecules. Various transparent media in order of decreasing velocity of light transmission and increasing refractive index are:

Table 2

Media	Light Velocity	Refractive Index
Aether	300,000,000 m/sec. (c)	1*
Air	<**	1.000277
Ice	<	1.31
Water	<	1.330
Pyrex	<	1.47
Acrylic glass	<	1.490-1.492
Crown glass	<	1.50-1.54
Amber	<	1.55
Diamond	<	2.419

*Scientifically defined as *light velocity in vacuum.*
**< meaning 'less than'.
Velocity in medium = c/refractive index, i.e. velocity of light
in diamond would be calculated as 'c ÷ 2.419'.

On Striking a Surface: Sound waves travelling in air cause
sensitive surfaces to vibrate. That is how we hear sound—by it
vibrating the sensitive eardrum diaphragm. The energy of the
sound is transferred to the surface that it strikes, and
sufficiently sensitive surfaces pick up that vibration. So, what
happens when a *light wave* strikes a surface? When sunlight
strikes a surface, its energy is likewise transferred; this causes
*the atoms of the surfa*ce to vibrate faster which registers as
heat. So whether it is sound or sunlight that meets a surface
the effect is really very similar—energy is transferred, with
attendant vibration. It is only the scale of the operation that is
different—*very* different. Atomic vibrations are of course less
than microscopic compared to surface vibrations. But of
course, a surface may either reflect or absorb, depending on
physical parameters such as rigidity and colour.

<u>Reflecting Surfaces:</u> Mirrors are of course good reflectors of light, while sound waves are reflected by surfaces that are hard, flat and rigid. Both light and sound obey the same law pertaining to reflection: 'Angle of incidence = angle of reflection'. If sending signals by means of a mirror, this becomes immediately apparent. The same basic law seems to apply to all wave motion, whether light, electromagnetic waves in general or a sound wave. But in addition to reflection, there are other criteria to consider, such as the pressure exerted upon a surface when a wave strikes it.

<u>Wave Pressure upon a Surface:</u> Regarding sound, what is referred to as 'subjective sound pressure level' is normally measured in decibels and decibel meters are available for this purpose. But the actual 'mechanical pressure' on a surface is measured in pascals (named after Blaise Pascal who lived in the 17th century). A pascal is equivalent to 1 newton (unit of force) per square metre. Measured pressure values range from 200 pascals for the sound of a jet aircraft at 50 metres to 0.02 pascals for normal conversation at 1 metre and 0.000063 pascals for distant rustling leaves. So *all* audible sounds exert a pressure but we are only really aware of the sound pressure from the more sudden or extreme events. So what about sunlight? Does that waveform also exert a pressure? It does, but the pressure exerted by sunlight, as one might sense, is very much less; and although negligible in our everyday living, it can nevertheless be calculated as a real value from Maxwell's equations. And Johannes Kepler in 1619 had correctly reasoned that it is the radiation pressure from the sun that directs a comet's tail *always away* from the sun. Quite so, and an excellent illustration! Scientists sometimes like to think of sunlight as 'photons' (little packets of energy) and the light pressure relates to 'photon flux' (Φ); that is 'photons per unit

area per sec'. [We can blame Newton for initially introducing the term 'flux'; that means 'flow', from the Latin, to describe his 'fluxions'—now, in mathematics, called calculus.] But the expression 'photon flux' is now used to calculate the number of electrons (current) produced by a solar cell. So perhaps, following the development of solar cell technology, light pressure *does* actually have its significance in our everyday living after all! And the pressure due to light *reflected from* a surface is always double that for *absorbed* light. It is clear from this discussion therefore that both sound and light exert measurable pressures when they fall upon a surface.

Law of Refraction: We know that there is a direction change when light passes from air into water—from a less dense medium to a surface that is more dense. This is of course why fish in a stream *seem* to be in the wrong position. Snell's law describes this in the scientific language. The law is said to be named after the 17th century Dutch astronomer Willebrord Snellius, would you believe, although first described by the scientist Ibn Sahl in Baghdad in 984. But perhaps 'Snell' is less of a tongue twister than either Willebrord Snellius or Ibn Sahl! Anyway, Snell's law relates the angles (to the normal— or vertical in the case of water surface), light velocity and refractive index:

$$\textbf{Sin } A_1 / \textbf{Sin } A_2 = \textbf{Velocity}_1 / \textbf{Velocity}_2 = \textbf{Refractive index}_1 / \textbf{Refractive index}_2$$

Although sound refraction is encountered less in our everyday situations, it does indeed still happen in the same way as with light. In ultrasound medical investigations and remedial work there are tissue boundaries to be considered, and it is clear that Snell's law is obeyed at these boundaries—for example, the boundary of bladder wall and urine. In seismic work, the course of sound waves is followed in Earth's interior where Snell's law is obeyed as different layers are crossed. It is deduced from seismic study that while the outer layer of Earth's core is liquid, the inner core is solid. So very clearly sound, ultrasound and light are all subject to the same law of refraction.

Doppler Effect: The motion of a sound source, the medium through which it travels and the listener, are relative. This means that the sound heard from an approaching vehicle siren will have a shorter wavelength than after it has passed by—heard by us as a higher note on approach than when the vehicle is receding. The change in the note heard is known as the Doppler Effect, named after the Austrian physicist Christian Doppler who stated the principle in 1842. And if the sound source travels faster in air than 343 metres/sec then the sound generated gets left behind. This is why the approach of a WW II, V2 rocket, would be heard *after* its detonation. But what about the light wave—does light also display this property? And how would we observe it? Doppler had correctly predicted that the effect should be common to all waveforms and suggested that it might account for the observed redness of some distant stars. His prediction was correct and we now have the term 'cosmological red shift'. If the universe is expanding, then distant stars/galaxies will be moving away so that to an Earthly observer the EM wavelengths will be lengthened. The lengthening of the waves means that the colour seen will be shifted towards the red end of the spectrum. Red shifts are now known with some precision (by reference to characteristic elemental absorption spectra). It was Edwin Hubble who noticed a rough correlation between red shift values and the distances of receding galaxies. So Doppler was perfectly correct and once again we see an essential property of light wave and sound wave as highly comparable.

Standing Waves: When a sound wave is reflected from a surface at 90^0 to direction of travel, then we have the situation of two physical waves occupying the same space and moving in opposite direction. The result is 'wave interference' and an emergent wave shape that has nodes and antinodes that appear to be standing still or static. So what? Well, all our music is based on precisely this—vibrating strings and vibrating columns of air inside tubes. Whether pop group, marching band or symphony orchestra, it all comes down to standing waves; leading to 'favoured frequencies', 'harmonics' and pleasant listening. So our music relies quite heavily upon standing waves. Let us then ask the question: Do light waves also exhibit a standing wave situation? Affirmative—they do! But again of course, on a much, much finer scale. Heinrich Hertz built an apparatus with which he was able to demonstrate how light reflected from a metal mirror can interfere with the original beam to form a standing wave. And the laser has been developed from in-step light wave reinforcement—**L**ight **A**mplification by **S**timulated **E**mission of **R**adiation. The laser device has a pair of facing mirrors and employs a crystal as a gain/reinforcing medium. Lasers have a number of technical and medical uses of course and can also be used to produce colourful light displays. So both light and sound are able to form standing waves.

Wave Guides: The principle of confining sound waves within a tube for their guidance has been around for quite a long time, and we are all well familiar with the wave guide principle as used in the medical practitioner's stethoscope. But humans are not the only species to make use of wave guides— which also occur in nature. There is a layer in the oceans known as the SOFAR Channel—**So**und **F**ixing **a**nd **R**anging Channel. In the oceans, temperature decreases and pressure increases with depth, resulting in a layer of ocean water in which sound velocity is at a minimum. The depth of this layer might well be 1,000 metres but it varies with location. The layer so formed acts as a wave guide, keeping (especially low notes) from dispersing, and sounds travel very much further. The fin whale makes good use of this SOFAR Channel and is able to communicate across thousands of miles of ocean. So the SOFAR channel is one example of a naturally occurring wave guide. Some fishermen will be aware that a comparable wave guide situation can occur over a lake in the early morning. A layer of cool moist air will stay with the lake while the sun's rays warm the upper air, creating an atmospheric layer. In this situation, people on either side of the lake can speak with each other across a really surprising distance with no need to shout.

Manufactured wave guides for light come under the heading of 'fibre-optics'. Glass fibres can act as wave guides, so that light is conveyed along a bundle of fibres from source to wherever it is required. This is a simple use but there are also much more complex engineering uses. Typically, glass fibres a little thicker than a human hair, are coated with a plastic of lower refractive index and bundled to make a fibre optic cable. Such cables can carry huge amounts of information as light signals over great distances, and are more efficient in a number of ways than the more familiar current-carrying *metal* cables. So once again we see a similarity; both light and sound waves readily respond to wave guide applications.

Discussion and Inferences: Sound and light, although we sense them in very different ways, are nevertheless both *wave forms* and as such are seen to obey exactly the same universal laws that apply to all waves. We currently understand sound waves rather better than light—probably because, like our physical selves, sound is of the material world. Sound is generated within the material world from a vibrating material source and is transmitted through a physical medium. It is a 'mechanical' process that buffets the air so that adjacent populations of molecules/particles get alternately compressed and rarefied; and the wave goes on its way through the air at 343 metres/sec. Light and other EM waves are generated in much the same way but on a vastly different scale. We can think of light as being generated by vibrating atoms/ions buffeting the aether. The aether vibrations that emerge from our sun—that is our sunshine for example; and the light waves go on their way out across the universe at 300,000,000 metres/sec. But the aether is essentially smooth and not particulate, so its intrinsic character will be that little bit different from air. But perhaps we should also consider air to have a measure of smoothness—this due to its molecules interacting to a sufficient degree, thus conferring that little bit of elasticity. While air has its small measure of elasticity, by comparison, we might see aether as having *perfect* elasticity. Perhaps therefore it comes as no surprise that the two waveforms have such a great deal in common. We might even consider the possibility that light, like sound, is a form of 'compression wave' but in a *perfectly* elastic aether medium. If this is so, then it would seem very likely that compression (or twisting or movement of some kind) within the medium relate to what Maxwell describes as magnetic and electric vectors of the travelling waveform. In any case, the very existence of electric and magnetic vectors requires explanation. Maxwell has eloquently demonstrated how they link to each other and we can clearly see that they can only have been generated *from* the aether by the travelling light wave, and this has itself been generated by the buffeting of atoms/ions against aether. So, by comparing light wave with sound wave in respect of universal laws we have learned something about that *fifth element*. As it carries light across the universe it somehow becomes *distorted* into electric and magnetic components—finally giving up its energy at the end of its journey when it comes into contact with matter once again. So, we could even think of aether as having a role as 'haulier', humping energy across the universe from one vibrating material location to another.

Before moving on, there is one further phenomenon that deserves our mention: that is a phenomenon known as sonoluminescence—the conversion of sound wave into light wave. Yes, this is actually possible. The phenomenon has been known since 1933-4, with much further study from 1990 onwards. In a typical experimental arrangement, a tiny gas bubble is placed in a flask filled with water that is subjected to a 20 KHertz resonance. It is found that when exactly centred, the tiny bubble rhythmically implodes and expands and produces light. Various theories have been postulated to explain this, but the firmly established fact is: sound and light are inter-convertible, so that this again points to their very close similarity. And it might even be said that a tiny zone that rhythmically expands and implodes could have some semblance to a unit forming part of a compression wave. Perhaps there is food for thought here.

CHAPTER 6 – COSMOLOGY FROM COSMIC EGG TO BIG BANG

Thoughts about the cosmos, its origin and its development, have continued across the more recent Earthly millennia for which we have records. The Rig Veda, the oldest of sacred Hindu books (15th – 12th century BC) names 'Brahma' as creator and describes the universe as 'Brahmanda'—*cosmic egg*. This was said to yield a cyclic universe, expanding from a 'Bindu' or point source, to its full maturity then return again to a point source. The cycling is said to continue endlessly. Why?—for what purpose? But the notion of a 'point source' has a familiar ring to it! So maybe we could see the Rig Veda cosmic egg version of the creation story as forerunner to the 'Big Bang' that has been the favoured theory of scientists throughout the 20th century. But again, we might ask: for what purpose? The Avesta record of Zoroastrian tradition, in-keeping with other theories, has a lot of big words, naming 'Ohrmazd' as creator who is said to be from the *place of endless light*—this according to the 'Mazdayasnian' religion.

In 5th century BC Greece, a materially objective style of thinking emerged. In addition to the inspired Pythagoras there was Anaxagoras who believed the original state of the cosmos to be different—a primordial mixture of ingredients. This was getting a small way perhaps towards the notion of an aether half-way stage. Democritus and Leucippus pursued atomic theory—seeing everything as comprised of indivisible units called 'atoms'. These indivisible units would have variety of size and shape, also the ability to move. And the atoms would require space in which they are able to move—a void. But it was the assertion of Parmenides that void is in reality 'nothing' and it is impossible for nothing to have existence; the space cannot be *completely* void, it must contain something, for example light—an interesting observation!

Unfortunately, the atomists of the day ignored the Parmenides insight. But seeing the cosmos as comprised of atoms that must have movement was of course a big step forward and most praiseworthy. Aristotle had been a student of Plato and he in turn, a student of Socrates—all three were great minds who did much to establish logical scientific reason. Aristotle wrote papers and lectured at the Lyceum—originally a speaker's corner and gymnasium (school). He established the 'Lyceum School' there. His followers were known as 'Peripatetics' on account of the way Aristotle would walk to and fro, whilst lecturing. But this one did such a great deal to promote and firmly establish the four elements/media—with a fifth element/medium being the aether.

The Stoic school that followed in the 3rd century BC held the belief of a finite universe in an infinite void, but taught that all is connected; also that errors in judgement lead to emotions that are destructive, and one's resolve should always be in accord with nature. Aristarchus must be credited with being the first to understand and describe the heliocentric solar system, this step forward also being made in that 3rd century BC. He accurately described the Earth as turning daily about its axis and orbiting annually about the sun, together with a sphere of fixed stars. But as with Parmenides, his insight was shelved in favour of Earth being at the centre of things.

Amazingly, this erroneous and seemingly egocentric belief would remain unchanged until the input of Nicolaus Copernicus, 1800 years later! Even then there was throughout Europe, an enormous reluctance to accept heliocentricity. Earth-at-the-centre had been the widespread belief for such a long time and it had suited the church to foster that belief. The Italian philosopher Giordano Bruno had supported the Copernican view, adding that our solar system is relatively insignificant and even the solar system is not at the centre of the universe. And this great scientist with his insight was burned at the stake by the Inquisition for stating his truth! The German mathematician and astronomer Johannes Kepler added the refinement of *elliptical* planetary orbits in 1605. Galileo became a supporter of heliocentricity and was put under house arrest for his supposed heresy in 1633—again by that wayward Inquisition that was responsible for so much disservice and suffering. And following the Copernicus publication, it was then more than one hundred years, taking us well into the 17th century, before the truth of heliocentricity found general acceptance! Since those muddled times there have been many more observations in astronomy and much further thought as to the structure and workings of the universe; leading us to what has become known as the 'Big Bang' theory, prevalent throughout the 20th century.

Big Bang Theory: Throughout the 20th century there have been the two opposing theories—'Big Bang' and 'Steady State', the former having by far the greater following. The work of UK astronomer Fred Hoyle and two Austrian scientists, Thomas Gold and Hermann Bondi, seemed to point to a steady state universe—one that expands, but while matter increases in it, overall density continues constant. But then, from Einstein's General Relativity equations, an expansion-from-point-source theory was deduced; this by Georges

Lemaître, a Belgian physicist and Roman Catholic priest—with the title 'Monsignor' bestowed by Pope John XXIII in 1960. This was quite a turnabout for the church from that aggressive and flawed unscientific attitude of earlier times—a big step forward! And strange as it may seem, the actual term 'Big Bang' was coined by Fred Hoyle in a BBC radio program when he referred to the non-Steady State theory as '...this big bang idea'. The name stuck. And Lemaître's Big Bang calculations seemed to point to the universe exploding/expanding from a point source/'singularity' 13.798 billion years ago. Strong support for universe expansion came from Edwin Hubble's Law—the observed red shift correlation with the distances of light sources as seen out across the universe. The discovery in 1965 of a cosmic microwave background radiation, considered to be left over from the Big Bang, was also cited as supporting evidence. And so this became the theory favoured by mainstream science throughout the 20th century. And the major supporting evidence was considered to be Hubble's Law—the red shift correlations—the Doppler effect as light travelled to our planet from afar.

A major event during the period of allegiance to Big Bang was the launching of the Hubble Space Telescope in 1990. This is a telescope of a modest 2.4 metres that is now in orbit nearly 600 km above our atmosphere. Being without any of the atmospheric distortions, it can transmit very high-resolution pictures and accurate spectra to Earth. It is also a means of observing in the near-infrared and ultraviolet light that otherwise get filtered out by our planetary atmosphere. It has been found useful to be able to 'see' in the various wavelength regions. So the Hubble Space Telescope is a really excellent device that now continually adds much more refined detail to our astronomic data. In particular we now have knowledge of the important fact that there are black holes at the heart of all large galaxies. This is a key fact to note. But a cyclic Big Bang theory continues to be the belief of mainstream science. So in going from Cosmic Egg to Big Bang, we might say one has travelled full circle! But let us not overlook the fact that this theory has been the product of purely *materialist* thinking, aided by a number of clever mechanistic contrivances. Whilst this work input clearly has a considerable value, a connection to spirit has simply not been sought and neither does the thinking observe the existence of aether. These are fundamentally grave errors that we must overcome. So how do others of an entirely different stance regard our strictly material scientific view?

Others?—well let me now properly introduce the irrefutable information source that is our enormous privilege to know— the one we know as Salumet, who visits from Angelic Realms. Leslie Bone, living in Kingsclere, UK, had received promptings from spirit to gather together a séance group that would meet weekly. That established group would include Eileen Roper who at that point in time possessed the rare capability to develop further as a *full trance medium—full trance* equating to a *pure channel,* with Eileen's consciousness placed entirely to one side during the séance sessions; this to suit a direct Angelic Realm link. Eileen's larynx would be used for speech by Salumet while her mind was away and incapable of moderating the message in any way. Then, with stage duly set, Salumet first joined with us (as had been previously disclosed) from spirit, on 27th June 1994. We felt so privileged and had so many questions to ask. Splendid! But one month later, Eileen had a virus and was not with us, and of course neither was Salumet—a splendid opportunity as it turned out for another to drop by and tell us a little about the mission. His words included the phrases:

~ *"This power which lately has been used for speech, is also used for the greater good of your world ... without such as yourselves, this work, this information, could not be broadcast."*

So, there we have it. This communicator went on to stress the huge importance of the new channel—this new link to the one of all-knowledge—Salumet—and we were thanked for our participation. The following week, 1st August 1994, Salumet was describing Earth as a planet of learning and a very, very minor part of this universe, which of course it is. And he made reference to this universe as 'the cosmic teaching house'. Yes, he actually describes the universe in its entirety as a *cosmic teaching house*. And through the next two decades of his ongoing mission it was to become clear to everyone exactly what he means by this. But following Salumet's reference to the universe, Leslie had jumped straight in with a question about the Big Bang and how we are told by scientists that the universe expands, to which Salumet gave a very quick reply:

~ **"How can they know? How can they know about the whole of the universe? They cannot. They are correct in part (but) what they are talking about is a very small part of the whole."**

It is of course an apt point and a piece of basic logic—even with the Hubble space telescope, our range of vision remains severely limited and we can only see a tiny part of this universe. To illustrate his meaning, he compared the universe to a sand dune of which we can only see a few grains—and what happens when the wind blows? Leslie had to agree that we in fact have no conception at all as to the full magnitude of

71

the universe but continued to pursue the point about expansion:

~ **"Yes—yes, movement, vibration, energy—yes, you have it my friend. It is always moving—it is never static."**

Leslie referring to a previous session in which 'energy' and 'thought' were declared to be the dominating factors within the universe:

~ **"Yes—yes. *That* is the true expansion."**

So, the evolution of our minds and the energies are the really significant factors—not so much the cosmic hardware. I had then voiced acceptance that we can see but a small part, and suggested that the speed-of-light seems to limit our more detailed exploration, but with better understanding perhaps this should not be so:

~ **"Yes—let me say, you are indeed limited by what you know and understand. There are other galaxies ... let me say this to you: How do you suppose that there are space travellers if they do not travel quicker than the speed of light as *you* know it? That must answer your question ... the speed of light is only the Earth's conception of speed. There are many things that the Earth is not aware of—but you will become more and more knowledgeable in these matters as time progresses."**

How very true! At the time we did not latch onto the full meaning of those few carefully chosen words. But now, nearly 30 years of teaching onward, an evolved website and five published books later, we have become a little more knowledgeable—not *just* from Salumet's teaching, but from discussions with actual space travellers—extraterrestrial sentient beings whose visits have been arranged for us *by* Salumet. But then that has been all a part of the teaching program, one might say! In particular, there have been 80 highly informative exchanges with 'Bonniol' and his large séance team on Planet Aerah, via Paul—Bonniol's chosen medium. And indeed, as has been stated, it is minds and energies that are important in this universe—that has now, as one result of these exchanges, become crystal clear to us. In fact, we now know that in the trance state, our wonderful brains can *download thought-behind-words to their known language*, and this is the factor that makes such communications possible—bypassing what might otherwise be seen as an impossible translation task! And we now know of two formats used by others to travel in excess of light velocity—there may well be more. And one further statement has been made on the Big Bang by Salumet:

~ **"It rather indicates to me that there is a higher being who suddenly says: 'Let us make a Big Bang!' It does not make sense to me, and so I have to say that I would reject that way of thinking."**

By 25th April 2005 Salumet had introduced us to the ET-communications and I was declaring how this had really brought home to us, on account of the instantaneous nature of the communications that spirit is without space or time.

~ **"Yes. Always this has been a difficult subject for you but we do feel that by this example you are now ready to receive and to accept that there is much more than you at first recognized."**

And indeed I now realized something about that Big Bang faux pas that had not occurred to me in our discussion of ten years earlier; so I placed a question concerning this:

Q: "Could I just refer back to that distant time in the past when we mentioned 'Big Bang' theory, and in relation to that scientists came up with the idea of a 'singularity', and the singularity would be visualized as a point-without-space-or-time, and of course the singularity as conceived—was viewed in *physical* terms. But if that singularity were viewed with *spiritual* eyes—without space or time—it might well be seen as spirit. So perhaps the scientist's only mistake was to view the idea of absence of space or time with physical eyes instead of with spiritual eyes?"

~ **"Yes. You are correct with your thinking. After all, many things that happen upon your planet have been because individuals have seen life through physical eyes rather than seeking the spiritual explanation. That is true in many aspects of your living, even in the way that you view your own planet. For so long individuals could see nothing other than what stood before them, but all that is changing ... gradually mankind has awakened to the spiritual aspect of all life. And after all, remember that spirit has always been, and whatever explanation mankind considers it cannot change the ultimate truth."**

I had replied: "Spirit has always been, as you have told us—"

~ **"No matter what words or discussions are used within your scientific community, it cannot be altered; no matter** which words are used, which intelligences are embarked upon.”

I reflected that it now seems almost amusing that what we call a *singularity* should simply be seen as *spirit*—and spirit has always been!

~ **“Yes, it seems so simple does it not, when you speak your words but to many it has not appeared to be so simple.”**

I had replied: “No, because we have been so *intellectual* and so *physical*.” Whereupon Salumet finally concluded:

~ **“Yes. I would say to you, each one of my dear friends: think simply as does the small child. When they look for explanations, it comes from *within*, and that is where the truth lies—deep from within.”**

So perhaps it is appropriate that our 20th century foray into increasingly complex physical reasoning should be brought to a close. The entirely physical approach appears to have spawned an erroneous Big Bang theory; but we should observe nonetheless that much valuable ground has been covered along the way, and many interesting ideas and facts have emerged. But the scientific mainstream has to acknowledge spirit and must involve the aether stage of the creation process in its further considerations, or it clearly cannot usefully move any further forward.

The substance of Einstein's 1920 lecture surely points quite firmly towards aether acceptance providing the logical stance. The details listed in chapter 5, comparing the character of light and sound waves are consistent with this key fact, and this in turn is consistent with a 'steady state' universe that did not begin with a big physical bang.

CHAPTER 7 – STEADY STATE UNIVERSE THEORY

S *teady State Universe:* 'Steady State' cosmology was developed as an alternative proposition to a 'Big Bang' theory, initially developed by James Jeans in the 1920s. This theory was later updated in 1948 by James Jeans, Thomas Gold and Hermann Bondi—it depicts a seemingly unchanging universe with no beginning and no end. But later discoveries seemed to suggest that changes are in fact occurring. Discoveries of quasars and radio galaxies existing only at great distance, suggested to inquiring intellect that changes have indeed occurred; also the discovery of cosmic microwave background radiation—this was deemed to have been left over from the Big Bang. These observations were influential in getting cosmologists to abandon any further consideration of a steady state, as it was at that time envisaged. But as the years rolled on, further carefully conducted experiments produced more facts that would eventually lead to a rather different formatting of steady state cosmology. But perhaps we should keep in mind that the salient meaning of our description of 'steady state' is that the universe is without beginning and without end—it is just permanently ongoing. In fact, during one of our earlier séance meetings, dated 22nd August 1994, Salumet had answered a searching question from Leslie with a reply that aligns to this view:

~ **"As far as I am aware, I do not know of a beginning, I only know that it has always been and always will be. That is the state of the teaching as I know it—I can only say of what I know. But as far as I am aware there has been no beginning as such. I am aware of what you are speaking of. I am aware of the talk of 'Big Bang' and all the other things. But I can only state to you: as far as I am aware, there has been no beginning as such."**

Well, there we have it, and it is therefore appropriate that we thoroughly investigate the further work that has been conducted in regard to the 'Steady State' theory of a universe that issues from and is dependent upon the omnipresent aether for its continuation.

So let us see the aether in its true context—see it as being absolutely everywhere and in contact with absolutely everything that has physical existence; while at the same time everything physical remains totally dependent upon it for its upkeep. Let us also observe that all material bodies in the universe are moving—spinning, orbiting and are being drawn by gravitational forces. It seems logical to suppose that there are interactions between it and moving bodies, and that the aether within itself must have something akin to movement. But the latter would not be immediately apparent to us on account of its non-material nature. But it is clear that whatever motions prevail and whatever interactions occur, the general situation is bound to be highly complex as observed by present day humanity. And then there is the passage of light and all other EM waveforms. It transmits or is a carrier of visible light and those other waveforms, called by various names according to waveband properties and usage. The red shift has already been mentioned, and at this stage we might see this as evidence for movement within aether's vast omnipresence—the movement away from Earth equating to an apparent lengthening of waves as observed. So it is reasonable and rational that we look to light and similar EM waveforms as tools to be used in our further studies.

In 1991, Roland De Witte conducted a 'detection of aether flow' experiment that yielded a significant result. His conceptual approach was refreshingly different from earlier work. In simplified explanation his experiment amounted to this: A radio frequency EM signal was sent along a copper coaxial cable of 1.5 Km length. The cable was aligned north-south and the signal sent in both directions (north → south as well as south → north). There was an observed difference in travel times and the measurements were continued for 178 days—178 Earth rotations. The observed difference in travel times was found to vary with the Earthly rotation, and this was seen to relate to *sidereal* time and not to solar time. [A sidereal day is slightly shorter than our 24-hour calendar day, with Earth's rotation being measured with respect to a distant star. At the end of a cumulative 178-day period there would be a 12-hour difference between calendar day counting and sidereal day counting.] It was possible from this to assess the direction of aether-flow with respect to Earth in addition to the aether-velocity. So a positive value for velocity was obtained

79

and the flow was seen not to relate to solar system movement but beyond it—to *galactic* movement. Furthermore, these results were seen to be in agreement with a previous set of results recorded by US physicist and astronomer Dayton Miller, conducted on Mount Wilson in 1925-6. That had been one of several experiments conducted as follow-up to the Michelson-Morley experiment that was given its null interpretation. Dayton Miller had used an optical interferometer for his experiment. So we now have agreeing data from two very different approaches conducted in two different countries! And furthermore, these findings have since (2001-2002) been confirmed in Ukraine by Uri Galaev. So there is very good reason to suppose that the unexpectedly small values obtained in the Michelson-Morley experiment may have been truly significant after all, while the null-conclusion drawn at that time was incorrect.

A Large-Scale Structure: The study of large-scale structure for the universe has been another major development in recent years to which many scientists have contributed. There have been team studies, conferences, much collaboration and several suggested models. The Voronoi model, named after Georgy Voronoi, a Ukrainian mathematician, is a mathematical device that can be used to make a general study of seeding distributions and how such distributions might lead to the formation of a cellular pattern. This model has been successfully applied to a study of universe large scale structure, as has been indicated by density and luminosity seed points. And the comparison of model with actual observed pattern has been a highly involved study. One scientist who has been central in all this and who has presented key papers is Estonian astrophysicist Jaan Einasto. The carefully deduced outcome is that the universe has a very large-scale *cellular* structure. There appears to be a number of huge cells, each many, many light-years across. The huge cells are virtually void of stars and matter; all galaxies of the universe being concentrated at cell wall locations—those regions where cells meet, especially in those regions where *several* cells meet. At these locations there are galaxies that have been named 'nodal super-giants'. And recent observations now indicate that there are galaxies and clusters of galaxies—known as 'super-clusters'. So the large scale structure of the universe would appear to be a 3-dimensional lattice made up of galaxies, each cell of the lattice being a vast volume that is void of galaxies. And there is reason to suppose that this large-scale structure is extremely slow to change, so that what is currently observed is also some indication of earlier evolutionary history. It is therefore suggested that the cosmic cell pattern, in addition to being its present status, is indicative of an early stage of universe development. These various criteria, when pieced together, have then led to the development of what is now termed 'DSSU theory'.

Dynamic Steady State Universe (DSSU): The Big Bang theory dates from the work of Friedman and Lemaître carried out in the 1920s, and today many adherents have remained reluctant to move away from that stance; this because it would mean that a century of wrong thinking must be acknowledged! A huge change of direction would of course follow, with scrapping of old ideas and replacing with new. The notion that all that we can observe and much, much more suddenly explodes from one singularity speck as source, to yield an ever-expanding universe with its boundary continually moving into an unknown nothingness—well, that was always a shaky proposition, and imponderable questions had been arising at every turn of intellectual inquiry. But the more recent realization of a universe having a large-scale cellular structure would appear to have opened a much-needed door towards a more rational concept of cosmology.

Conrad Ranzan, DSSU Research, Niagara Falls, Canada has pieced together what is termed a theory for a Dynamic Steady State Universe (DSSU), (2002). This theory acknowledges and embodies the omnipresence of aether, the 3-dimensional cellular cosmic structure and flowing aether movements, with some description of the latter. It is postulated that aether expansion within the huge cosmic cells yields an outflow from cell centre towards each cell periphery. Towards and within the vicinity of cell periphery there is *apparent* aether contraction; such that the overall effect of expansion and contraction yields a steady state universe that does not expand—the size of each cell is unchanged and overall universe size continues steadily constant. But what about the observed red-shift that is described as increasing with distance as we view from Earth across the universe? Do the aether expansions and contractions cancel out? A mathematical treatment seems to indicate that there is no cancellation. In the Dynamic Steady State Universe, red-shift relates quite simply to space/aether expansion (within cell limits), which is not the same as total universe expansion. But aether expansion as opposed to contraction somehow wins red-shift-wise. This might well be due to the aether being swallowed up by matter as opposed to contracting. The opposite of red-shift is blue-shift (consistent with aether contraction). It seems that there is a detectable blue-shift component where cell meets cell but this is small compared to observed red-shift *across* each cell. It is pointed out that DSSU theory complies with the Copernican Principle (named after Nicolaus Copernicus and referring to sun-centred heliocentricity) and with a perfect Cosmological Principle. The latter refers to universe isotropy (in large scale observation from Earth, the universe appears the same in all directions) and to homogeneous character (the same everywhere).

To place Big Bang theory on the scrapheap of yesterday's ideas and transfer allegiance to DSSU, certainly suits extremely well the profound teaching received from spirit; also, following that, the discussions we have had with several informative sentient beings in spirit. You will recall that at the outset we spoke of a threefold basis of creation:

Spirit > Aether > Materialized Universe

Logically, there have to be locations or regions in space where such conversions or transmutations are taking place. It would appear from DSSU-detail that the creation of aether from spirit has to take place within the huge cells, resulting in their expansion; it is also consistent with their absence of material content. Transmutation of aether into materialized universe clearly takes place in those regions where cell boundaries meet—in the regions where galaxies abound. The various material bodies at those locations will require aether for their ongoing upkeep, consistent with a flow of aether into each, creating a general picture of aether flow-dynamics; also accounting for what we call 'gravitational forces'. As to the precise locations of matter creation within the cell-boundary/galaxy network, that remains unclear from scientific endeavour at this stage. But there has been word from spirit sources on that and that subject will be dealt with as we move on.

Process Physics: Reginald Cahill, Flinders University, Adelaide, Australia takes us further forward; with much recalculating of earlier work, conducting further evaluations and then piecing it all together. And this approach leads to a complex but logically acceptable picture. There is recourse to equations and mathematical treatment of results, which of course today's institutions require as evidential proof. Referring back to Newton: Newton had acknowledged existence of 'space' but not its dynamics, and so had rated space as unobservable. Einstein on the other hand, saw 'space' as a 4-dimensional construct with time; hence the term 'space-time'. Space in this context was deemed to be dynamic, and as we have seen since Einstein's work was published, gravitational lensing—the dragging of space as the result of planetary rotation and gravity's influence on the red shift phenomenon, are each supportive of Einstein's reasoning. This is all very interesting, but it now seems unquestionably clear from a collective evaluation of recalculated results and the additional 21st century work, that aether dynamics abound and, within today's consciousness, are here to stay. It is clear that light speed is anisotropic—it is direction dependent. And it is pointed out that, despite some thinking otherwise, Einstein's special relativity does *not* require light speed to be isotropic.

Cahill deduces from re-calculating the results of Michelson, Morley, Miller and others, an aether flow component of 420±30 Km/sec *through* the solar system, a 42 Km/sec inflow *to* the sun, and a 30 Km/sec flow past our planet by virtue of its orbital motion and skimming its surface tangentially (2002). [I would expect there also to be an inflow into the Earth but this might well be very much smaller by comparison.] He did further work (2006) using coaxial cable and EM-radio signal—as did De Witte; also using fibre optic cable and atomic clocks. Further details were obtained from these studies such that De Wittes' work has been corroborated and extended; and following the further analysis of Miller's gas-mode interferometer results, his work also was corroborated. The overall conclusion to be drawn from Cahill's experiments plus his scrutiny of all that earlier work is that aether does indeed exist; also it may be concluded that Earth's passage through that aether has been repeatedly demonstrated in experiments from 1887 onwards! It is also suggested that there is no longer any need for that erroneously conceived 'dark matter', and the dynamics of aether movement will account for that mysterious force that we know as 'gravity'. The reasoning of 'process physics' is quite complex and perhaps difficult to follow. But the point is well made within this genre that it opens the way forward to thinking beyond what might be described as a *strictly material existence*—this is the way that the details of existence have been viewed by scientific majority in our recent past; albeit some have come close to identifying this non-material essence of creation, calling it simply *space* or *quantum matter*, *zero-point field*, *quantum foam*, *Higg's ocean* etc.

It has now become crystal clear that the reality is so much more than just the material existence. Process physics signals the acceptance of a dynamic model for a non-material aether existence, which is seen as a *self-organizing* system. An important outcome from this reasoning is that gravity is seen as resulting from aether movement—as an inflow. We have already referred to the apparent slowing down of light in transparent materials (Table 2). It is deduced mathematically that this is a scattering effect with the actual light speed relative to aether remaining constant. That would seem to make good sense. Clearly, there have been really basic misconceptions throughout our 20th century, leading to an urgent need for correction. It is now time, as we move on from that period, for scientists to change direction and face up to re-thinking some basic concepts in cosmology, and indeed concepts in the whole of physics!

Concerning the discipline of 'physics', Cahill observes that equations such as those of Maxwell, Schrödinger and Dirac, that have been taught as bastions of learning and accepted in their totality, are not reflecting the influence from aether's dynamics. In this regard it is emphasised, and as has been intimated earlier, that Einstein's space-time is a mathematical construct and not an aspect of reality. But how does one express the non-material aether's interplay of streaming in various directions? Here Cahill himself employs a mathematical construct, whilst at the same time clearly stating that this is so. Employing this device also means that the notion of *space* stays with us—space being a word that, over the years, has become well-fixed in our thoughts and vocabulary, albeit not well defined. The multiple movements of aether zones are referenced to a 3-dimensional space background—a dynamic aether network embedded in a mathematical 3-dimensional space. Taking this step does seem to allow a mathematical treatment via equations thus enabling precise description. This can lead to data on the masses of black holes and to explanation of so-called 'dark matter effect' in spiral galaxies. And it would appear that a full description of gravity requires the Newtonian constant 'G' plus a dimensionless fine structure constant denoted by 'α'. All this has now become rather complicated and perhaps difficult to get one's head around—apologies!

Being very much impressed by such detailed endeavour, I drew Salumet's attention to Professor Reginald Cahill's work at our meeting of 23rd February 2015, beginning with his use of the term 'quantum foam'; while at the same time pointing out that the term 'aether' being out of fashion these days, authors tend to use other names so as to facilitate acceptance of their papers by peer-reviewed journals. His reply included:

~ **"Yes—whatever suits the mind of even one person, if it makes sense then that is fine..."**

He then added:

~ "I will speak from spirit when I say that there is much work going on in trying to understand your world and your universes. But I have to say, my dear friends, that it all has to become much more simple. Scientists are making things too complicated, because of their own logical minds."

But one has to observe that the intellectual thought pattern and detailed study seem to have become mandatory in science, otherwise one's voice is simply not heard. Our teacher continued:

~ "But it really matters not to us in spirit what they call something, as long as they eventually reach the spiritual aspect."

Ah! It is the spiritual—that elusive non-material aspect, that is important—quite so! I continued with: "I think you have told us the aether plays a role in up-keeping all matter in its various forms?"

~ "Everything is connected; that is the simplicity— everything is connected in some way or another."

I had replied to that: "And there seems to be evidence for the aether being drawn into bodies in the universe—or perhaps *'being drawn into'*; is the wrong expression—"

~ "Yes, I would not like to use it in that way, but I understand what you are saying and of course, all beings have to use the energies which are part of them, which is used for existence; no matter whether it is a human existence, a worldly existence or universal existence. That energy is common to *all* things."

So, all things as a necessity utilise the energy which is everywhere. Our teacher sees this as a simple truth, while some of us think of this more as a distribution.

I had replied: "Yes, and we talk about the connection to planets and suns—and to galaxies one might say—"

~ "NO!—you *must* say, not *might* say. You cannot exclude!"

And everyone had a really good laugh as my line of inquiry this time was quickly curtailed. Well, I know from past experience that Salumet is not forthcoming with information for mankind when it should be our task to discover for ourselves—that would defeat the object of our being here to evolve on a free will basis. Later, he was saying:

~ "But I do not like to dissuade people—to not think; because by thinking, even if you are mistaken, eventually you can come to the right outcome."

I said: "I feel there's been an awful lot of that *(not thinking)* in our scientific journey!"

~ "And much more to come of course, but all of these things are less important when you travel home (to spirit). You will eventually understand more, and wonder why all of these situations seemed so complicated!"

This and further commentary confirms the point that we are all making our science more complicated than need be. And I think we have to agree this point where the nature of gravity is concerned. Looking back to Galileo's experiment, when he dropped cannon balls and musket shot from the leaning tower—there was no difference in their travel times—no difference in the acceleration due to gravity. This was a simple experiment that said so much. If a feather is dropped, it will of course travel much more slowly than any metal object, but the reason for this is air resistance plus any wind effect. It has since been demonstrated that, in a vacuum, a coin and a feather fall with the same acceleration, consistent with each being caught up in the same flow. Perhaps this is difficult to imagine—we are so accustomed to living with the effects of air resistance.

An even simpler experiment concerns A A Milne's fictional character 'Pooh Bear', who played a favourite game of 'Pooh Sticks'. He and friends would throw their different sized pieces of stick into a stream and then rush to the downstream side of the bridge to see whose stick appeared first. All of course, regardless of size, were caught up in the same flow—but there might also be a fine structure effect, due in this context to an occasional eddy or a little weed deflection!

It may well be that the growing complexity of our science is becoming a burden that hampers us on our way forward—and that is the word we have from spirit. I feel that the attitudes of peer-reviewed journals and bodies responsible for project funding play their part in this. But nevertheless, I do admire the reasoning of process physics, and I feel that Cahill's description of aether dynamics comes much closer to the truth than has been conceived in our more recent past.

PART 3 – PYRAMID ENERGIES ARE PROOF

CHAPTER 8 – A MESSAGE FROM PYRAMID TECHNOLOGY

Perhaps before moving onto a discussion of the more rational view of cosmology, we should note that evidence for aether sweeping past the surface of our planet has been staring us in the face for literally thousands of years. I refer to the large ancient pyramids such as those that have stood on the Giza Plateau, Egypt for around 12,000 years. There are also much older and larger pyramids here in Europe near the town of Visoko, Bosnia—this area, with its two rivers, having been settled from very early times. Radio-carbon dating of the Bosnian pyramids indicates an age for them a little in excess of 30,000 years. They are technological triumphs that have been built by visiting extraterrestrials using their own specifications and their own methodology, albeit with friendly co-opted human assistance. But how can we be certain of this? Well, these facts have emerged from both our interplanetary communications as well as spiritual guidance received. Furthermore, the details received all fit together to form a logical pattern; and in any event we have to face up to the fact that humankind prevailing 30,000 years ago would not have had the capability to accomplish feats such as these, with their magnitude and their intricacies of impeccable design, even if today's equipment had been available. The Bosnian pyramids, and other such pyramids about the planet, have one pair of sides aligned exactly east – west, so that the leading face sweeps squarely into the aether as Earth rotates on its axis. This is by intention of course and has not come about as a matter of chance! When a pyramid is constructed in this way, energy is continuously produced both within it and around it; also an energy beam is produced that rises vertically from the pyramid apex. One might think of the arrangement as a cosmic dynamo. But the energy produced is not one with which either our mainstream science or humanity as a whole is familiar—not one that the majority would at present consider utilising. But it is energy *very* familiar to the visiting ETs who have relied upon it for their wellbeing whilst on our planet and to assist their space vehicle launch for the return journey home.

How do we know these details and how can we be certain? Although mainstream science has a record of being fairly hit-and-miss over the years, we have more recently become accustomed to validation work where this is concerned— checks being carried out by different teams in different locations, often with some modification of the experimental conditions that have been used. The checking of course helps to build confidence in discoveries made. But what about spirit communications; must we simply accept these at face value without any checks where these are concerned? No—in the case of a séance group such as we have, information can be brought together from a number of different sources—from physical beings living on other planets who are far more advanced than humanity, from actual builders of Earthly pyramids in the past who once lived upon another planet and who are currently progressing their lives in spirit, and last but by no means least, from our guide and teacher who has knowledge of all facts—Salumet. By 'more advanced physical beings' is meant: they are conversant with interplanetary communications, they have progressed beyond the naive abhorrent practice of warring, have developed spirituality and have mastered some of the aspects of space-travel. But before quoting from these interesting and most valuable sources, it will assist our understanding to know a little about the energy that exists in recently constructed pyramids that certain of Earth's scientists have actually built for the purpose of further study and usage. So much has been revealed as the result of this recent work, and we owe a debt of gratitude to two Russian scientists in particular—to Volodymyr Krasnoholovets for his study of the Giza pyramids and his theorizing with regard to the interaction of aether with the pyramids to produce energy; and to Alexander Golod for designing and building his glass fibre and plastic east-west orientated pyramids, thus providing opportunities for experiments to be conducted by scientists from a number of different nations. Initially, two quite substantial pyramids of heights 44 and 22 metres, the larger amounting to 55 tons, were built in 1990. By 2001 there were seventeen in Russia and Ukraine. By 2010 there were more than fifty around the world, mostly in Russia and Ukraine. Many projects have since been carried out by large numbers of distinguished scientists, with a number of most remarkable results. The list of reported pyramid energy effects includes:

➤ The bonds between water molecules are altered such that ice is no longer formed, even at ambient temperatures as low as -38° C. If the container is shaken or knocked, *then* it freezes.

➤ Structural changes have been noted for several materials.

➤ Seeds stored in the energy for just a few days produce much greater crop yield, generally 20-100% increase and in one instance an increase of 400% has been reported.

➤ Razor blades are sharpened. Krasnaholovets has shown by electron microscopy that the effect is real and compares with ultrasound polishing.

➤ Resistance of carbon materials is altered.

➤ Salinity and heavy metals contents of water are decreased.

➤ Radioactivity is decreased.

➤ Stored foodstuffs stay fresh longer.

➤ Crystals stored in the energy and then transferred to jails reduce crime rate.

➤ Pyramid-stored salt and pepper was given to 5000 prisoners. They exhibited much reduced violence and their general behaviour was improved.

➤ Viruses are inhibited and healing occurs.

➤ Tissue culture tests demonstrate increased survival of cell tissue after infection by viruses and bacteria.

➤ There are reports of cancer cures.

➤ Dead animals seem to dry out or mummify instead of rotting.

➤ The energy is relaxing and improves sleep patterns.

➤ Longevity is markedly increased as shown in trials with rabbits and rats.

➤ Extensive trials with animals show decrease in disease incidence.

➤ There is a decrease in breeding capability of viruses.

➤ Pathogenic strengths of viruses and bacteria are reduced.

➤ Diseased white mice had much improved survival rates.

➤ Human aura is brightened.

➤ Meditation and psychic abilities are enhanced.

➤ Patient's burns heal faster in the pyramid energy.

➤ The energy is found to combat alcohol and drug addictions.

➤ Immune systems of organisms are improved—blood leukocyte composition increased.

➤ Growth of plants in the vicinity of pyramids is increased in their early growth phase.

➤ Pyramids in the vicinity of oil wells reduce oil viscosity by as much as 30%, thereby significantly increasing production rate.

➤ It is claimed that in the vicinity of pyramids, seismic events are lessened in severity and extent.

➤ In the vicinity of pyramids, violent weather patterns seem to be decreased.

➤ A vertical column of energy rises from the pyramid apex that is clearly revealed by radar.

It is obvious from the 30 items listed that with the pyramid energy, we are truly blessed with a remarkable phenomenon that can be of huge benefit to future humanity. To the best of my knowledge at the time of writing (early 2015), here in the UK, none of this has been reported by our TV news media—equally no mention of the pyramid excavations in Bosnia, now into their tenth year; with *their* continued ongoing flow of energy. Sadly, this insouciance of withholding really newsworthy news is denying enormous benefits to society; for example, hospital burns and treatment centres built to pyramid specification would be a blessing for a number of patients with burns. Farmers could also benefit from much improved crop yields through idealized seed storage facilities. Where oil production is concerned, the Middle East producers have the advantage of moderately hot conditions that favour reduced viscosity of the crude oil and this means fast pumping. Russian oil fields, despite lower temperatures, have stayed competitive by using a pyramid array to lower oil viscosity. All such applications of pyramid energy are now within our grasp. At the moment, in order to keep up with news of this rapidly expanding field, one either has to search the Internet or go to books such as this. The younger generation is catching on while the elderly and those without computers or the time to browse remain uninformed. Surely, all of us deserve to have knowledge of this important development!

Salumet was questioned on the Egyptian pyramids in 1994 when he first came to us. He was able to say little at that time because of our unprepared status. Question-and-answer sessions across the 'divide' with Angelic ones were then so new to us! But the movement of massive stone blocks, made weightless by means of de-materialization followed by re-materialization to their original state *was* discussed. We were assured that this was indeed part of the methodology used in building the Giza pyramids and that this is seen as an obvious natural procedure used by beings who are versed in spiritual ways. And Salumet had added that the people of those earlier times were rather more spiritual than present day populations, having both a fuller understanding and a much more ready acceptance of others from across the universe. At our meeting of 5th May 2003, the stage was set for receipt of further details, and our teacher made it very clear that pyramids have been built as destination points by *extraterrestrial* visitors to Earth:

~ **"...who came from other worlds. The drawings you speak of within the walls came later—they came from man and man's assessment of what they should have been. We are speaking of two different things here. It is a topic which we can enter into again another time if you so wish, but you must not mix the original construction or dematerialization, with what you find on the inner walls of these structures. There has been a time lapse, and mankind has *not* been correct in his timing."**

98

So it is clear that the decorative cartouches on walls of the Great Pyramid at Giza came much later than the pyramid construction. They came as a man-made addition much later. And then three years after receipt of that helpful data—26th June 2006)—I had come to know of the modern Russian project and was able to ask our teacher about *that* matter:

Q: "I would like to refer to some work that Russian scientists have been doing very recently—Professors Golod and Krasnoholovets. They are good scientists and have been building quite large, hollow pyramids out of glass fibre and plastic, up to 44 metres high. They have conducted a number of experiments, and two of their interesting results are: firstly, that water as it cools to very low temperatures, -40ºC, doesn't freeze! And another factor: seeds kept within the pyramid for a period, then germinate to give a crop yield that is between 20 and 100% greater than would normally be."

I suggested that these would be energy effects and that the seed result in fact compares with that observed for seed recovered from crop circles[1]. So perhaps our awareness of energies is improving just a little! Salumet began by reminding:

~ **"If you go back to the time of the ancient civilizations, they were much more aware of energies than you are at this present time."**

---

[1] Crop circle artists have not helped researchers trying to investigate this area, though when you know what to look for, it's easy to separate the wheat *(genuine crop circles)* from the chaff. *(manmade hoaxes)* Many good books have been written, with overwhelming evidence—it is imperative that we read what researchers have written rather than relying on agenda-driven news outlets.

Well, I think that is self-evident, but the question had opened the door to further helpful statements from our teacher:

~ **"What is happening with your Russian friends and their pyramid experiments is not new knowledge but knowledge that has been *regained* and is now beginning to be understood by men of your time. The ancient Egyptians in your world—in particular that race—had much more knowledge of energy and vibration—and space travel. When you speak of the water which reaches certain temperatures and still does not freeze, it comes under the same energy. And I would say to you, your analogy—the experiments and your crop circles—are indeed related to that same energy. It is an energy not fully understood as yet but I have to say, many are being helped in this field so that the understanding is greater and these, what are termed 'mysterious happenings', can now be collected and collated. The energy used is indeed of a higher vibration than currently known in your world. But, do you remember my dear friends when I told you that 'sounds' have their own vibration and that one evening you made the sound within yourselves and you could *feel* that vibration within? In the same way, the shapes of many things have their own vibration. There are many people in your world now, who find benefit from being within the shape of pyramids, because of the energy which is created within. And if you think of the shape of the pyramid, you will begin to realize my dear friend that all lines reach to a pinnacle as if the energy is being drawn upwards to a higher vibration."**

100

Wonderful! So we now have crop-circle-energy comparison; also a sound vibration analogy! And we notice that Salumet is careful to distinguish between *knowledge regained* and *new knowledge, as yet unknown to mankind.* [*Knowledge regained*, would be knowledge now held as Akashic Record from earlier civilisations.] I had then added that radar detects a column of energy rising from a pyramid apex to a height of about 1,000 metres:

~ **"And beyond!—you will then find that the vibration becomes even finer. But that is something not to be understood at this time. It is important for your scientists in your world now to recapture knowledge long lost."**

So we have confirmation from Salumet of the radar-derived data. I added that meditation appears to be enhanced in the pyramid energy:

~ **"Of course!—because as the energy reaches and goes from the top of the head, what is happening?—it reaches for the pinnacle. Can you see?—because the energy is drawn upward and becomes even more refined? So, perhaps my dear friends this would be something for you all to consider this time: the shape of the pyramids and how the construction is ever upwards and perhaps I will hear your thoughts next time."**

Lilian observed that ancient pyramids are scattered all over our planet and Salumet responded that earlier people were more adept in their knowledge of these things. Graham asked if they had a name for the energy—not one that our teacher was able to give, but he added that they would have had a

101

name for their own use. We spoke of 'inertons' as being part of Prof Krasnoholovets' theorizing. Salumet had replied that to use a name may well assist, but names are really not important; but having the *feel* for these things and *having the knowledge* are the important factors. Different names of course will be used by different peoples, just as a matter of convenience in conversation. I pointed out that we recognize from the work done so far that the energy penetrates many things and alters their character in some way:

~ **"It is part of the scheme of life. It is *the unknown* to you as humans *at this time*. It is nothing extraordinary, in fact I would call it most ordinary."**

Yes, we would seem to have moved away from what should be seen as 'ordinary' or 'natural'. Finally, in conclusion I had added that the political relations between East and West are so improved now (2006), and this sharing of knowledge is a very nice thing that is coming from that.

~ **"As it should be, do you not agree?—mankind should be sharing with his brother, because all knowledge belongs to all people."**

Exactly!—all knowledge really belongs to *all* people. I added that we really appreciate the good work that these scientists are currently doing and thanked our teacher for his further commentary.

~ **"Yes, and I will look forward to the remarks brought to us next time. This is something which we must discuss a little more, now that the topic has been raised."**

And that has indeed been a key factor in the exchanges: we first need sufficient knowledge and aptitude for asking the questions, and then we need to be able to follow Salumet's reasoning—and then go home and think some more about it. So three weeks later, I was referring back to making a sound within ourselves and describing it as a 'micro sound'—a higher vibration than airborne sound. The pyramid shape would have a condensing effect—so there are two main aspects to the pyramid influence: the sound refining and the collecting-of-energy as the leading pyramid face sweeps into the aether. We also mentioned that differently sloping sides prevail—Egyptian pyramids involving *pi* ratio and the Russian ones involving the steeper *phi* ratio:

~ **"Of course, the shape dictates the way the sound vibrations become more refined—it reaches the point of not being audible to human ears. When you experienced the sound within yourselves, remind yourselves of what you then felt. Can you remember?"**

I replied that I felt an 'on-going resonance'.

~ **"Yes. What you should have felt was that sound energy being refined until you became unaware of the human form and you became as one with the sound energy. So you see, all shapes, all sounds go together and, after all: Is not the human form in some shape?—and where does the sound rise to? The sound will always rise to the pinnacle of the shape—to that point within the shape that allows that sound to vibrate at a higher degree."**

So with our selves it would rise to the top of the head. As the conversation moved on, Salumet was saying:

~ "There is so much that can be spoken about energies and while we speak of energies, my dear friends, have you become aware of the talking going on within your world of harnessing the waters of the seas? I did tell you previously that that was the way forward."

And of course we all liked the thought of a clean fuel-free energy from the sea!

Jan looked for confirmation that Egypt had been visited from another planet and wished to know if that other planet would have been the source of their knowledge:

~ "The knowledge was innate within them, which would make it easier (for them) to accept other cultures. Their knowledge was indeed far superior to anything on this planet at this time."

So it had indeed been a high point for that civilization. I had next referred to the fact that in addition to the overall structure there were further structures in granite and different rocks within the Egyptian pyramids to presumably further enhance and develop the energy:

~ "You are correct and this is something I will discuss with you when we have more people to listen. Yes, of course it is not only shape and sound but texture, and remember, as we have said, *all things* have their own vibration. You all, my dear friends, are nothing but vibration."

Jan inquired if the thought entertained by the ancient Egyptians had been to entomb their dead within a pyramid so that they could pass into spirit more freely—taking all their wealth with them:

~ **"That** (thought) **came to a later civilization, the knowledge of which we speak was innate within them."**

Lilian commented that one who had recently spoken with us, who had lived in Egypt during days of pyramid building, was aware of the energies in water and food:

~ **"As were all of those people—this knowledge belonged to all of that civilization. So you see it was normal to them, but gradually that knowledge was lost."**

So why was that knowledge lost?

~ **"Materialism was beginning to take hold—there are many, many reasons but the downfall of many civilizations was caused by man's own ego and although that seems too simple, that is the basis of many, many civilizations' downfalls—where mankind assumes a role of being the 'creator'."**

So Jan had then asked if that was down to mankind's freewill and is it a part of our evolution that we lose that ego to eventually come full circle:

~ **"—Both."**

Jan: "So the wealthier they became, the more gold they found—that became their downfall."

~ "And their beginning of abuse of all things spiritual. Mankind basically, in simple terms, has lost his way—but as you well know my dear friends—that is being reversed gradually in your world."

Jan: Haven't we come a long way spiritually in the last 100 years even?

~ "As human beings, let me say it to you this way: You have always been spiritual beings but you have been in the dark as far as *recognizing* those spiritual gifts—and perhaps 'gifts' would not be the correct word—they are innate within you but the recognition of who and what you are has been lost."

Clearly on reflection, there is still at present a minority who hold most of the world's gold and treasures and wield much power. But as the discussion continued it was agreed that change was indeed in progress but no, we have not yet come full circle, and Salumet added that he would not be here if that were the case, and there is much work still to be done! Finally, he summed up regarding his mission:

~ "I have to say my dear friends, apart from all of the other information given, the most important part of our coming to you, (is) that each one of you, whether it be within this group or within the many, many others throughout your world—it is to recognize and to know that you are spirit and that you have the abilities of spirit at your call."

Our teacher was again with us on 7th August 2006 and on this occasion was happy to speak further about the Egyptian pyramids, declaring that so much that has been written is incorrect. That fact can of course easily be surmised from reading the literature, so much of which is very clearly contradictory!

~ **"I know to this day there is much puzzlement. We have spoken recently about smaller versions of the pyramids** (the modern Russian structures) **and the energies which they contain within. But let us go back in time to that time when that Egyptian race should have been leaders of their time in the way of spirituality."**

I asked if that would have been the time of Osiris:

~ **"We go further back in time, when many from our world came to advise and to help this planet to become—I will use today's phrases for your understanding—to become more spiritual in nature. The people of that time had much knowledge within. They understood much of the way of nature in your world. Much was made of the earth, the fire, the air and all that was natural. They also had the abilities of spirit in as much as they recognised the transmutation of energies and how energy could be used to benefit mankind. They understood what man has now lost. I would say when first they began to build—and I say to you: the knowledge came to them from within, from that innate understanding—but it also came _to_ them from other beings from other planets. So, you understand my dear friends, how much knowledge they had before them**

as they began their structures. It was for the purpose of 'travel' and 'time' and to be in alignment with the sun and the planets at that time. The structures were not for, as used in later days, as burial mounds for their pharaohs. That comes later and I will explain a little to you. Within the structures that they built would be a chamber that would be used by all—man, woman, child and even the animals of that time. It was used like today's people would use your cathedrals; for upliftment, for healing and to gain knowledge. Within these structures there would be one who would be willing to teach, who had come to this planet for that very purpose. Therefore, these buildings were always in alignment to nature. And, as we have spoken briefly, the energy within the pyramids is most powerful. I will hesitate at this point for any questions that you may have—"

I gave the names of 'Osiris' and his queen 'Isis', and there was a son 'Horus', indicating that it was my information that these were the last of that biological line from elsewhere:

~ "Yes. That information is correct. That is why I said that we go further back because they were indeed the last in that line."

More was said on this occasion about the Pharaohs and their decline, those details being reported elsewhere[1]. And it was made clear that conditions were highly favourable for this ET-guided project in Egypt at this time; also that no other Earthly cultures were approached by them. This was a lengthy session with much more general information included. The energy was fading towards the end, and as Salumet departed, we were all left quite spellbound.

As intimated, knowledge of time and universe are key factors in space travel. Today, we are familiar with twelve zodiac signs. Those of ancient Egypt went further and their 'star clock' was divided into thirty-six star groups for their calendar. One full cycle of Earth's precession takes 25,920 years, so the stars get back into the same sync as seen from Earth just once in 25,920 years. And the beings of what has been termed *Egyptian mythology* are not mythic or imaginary entities at all, but *real* beings that once trod this Earth. It would be well that we take proper note of this increasingly clear fact. This period, during which aware humans accepted assistance from benevolent extraterrestrial visitors, should be seen as a firm corner stone of Earthly history. Hieroglyphs were developed into written language on the papyrus, right here in Egypt, and orientated pyramids swept the aether to provide a *real* energy that could be *felt*, appreciated and used to good purpose by the many. This was a truly splendid time in Earthly history—a lofty summit in our pathway forward.

CHAPTER 9 – PYRAMID ENERGY
CONFIRMATIONS: BONNIOL

The evidence presented thus far, for interaction between pyramids and aether has come from eminent Russian scientists and from the all-knowing Salumet. In addition, there are other sources that have corroborated the facts described. One most valuable source has been our dear friend 'Bonniol', a sentient physical being like ourselves—with two eyes, arms and legs but of larger size, more hairy, and who is certainly far more knowledgeable, loving and intelligent than humans on Earth today. Together with a large participating séance group, he lives on a planet known to their kind as Aerah, in a distant galaxy. It should be mentioned that in trance state when minds are linked, our wonderful brains (human, Aeran and others), can *download* the thought behind words to the brain's known language—brains may be thought of as the most incredible biological computers. We have enjoyed around eighty exchanges with Bonniol since 2004 when he first joined with us, all via Paul his chosen medium. We discovered quite early in the exchanges that Bonniol's people are familiar with the principle of de-materialization and utilise it in their own construction work:

~ "We can move objects of enormous size, and it is the vibrations that are changed to allow this to happen."

In the exchanges that followed, Bonniol extolled the virtues of mind and mind-control (6th June 2005):

~ "Mind is everything in some ways—projecting the mind— it is like sending yourself out, rather than a thought—"

Returning to the subject of construction work we asked about the *shaping* of blocks:

~ "There are methods of lightening the blocks. There are also methods for helping to shape them. They are different methods. We can make them more pliable—we can alter them with our thoughts."

Well, it has over the years become our understanding that thought is all-powerful and later Bonniol was saying:

~ "When you dematerialize the block of stone, it is possible to re-materialize it in any shape or form, if you have clarity of thought. You can manipulate or change anything with thought, if your thoughts are strong and clear enough. There are no boundaries."

So we now have understanding of how it was possible for those who built the Giza pyramids to achieve what seems to us today to be impossible precision—the excellence of fit has always been a problem for present-day Egyptologists and scientists alike to comprehend. And this information is of course consistent with the extraterrestrial input.

Our ET-friend went on to confirm that there are many planets in the universe that have life—not always as we might expect it to be, and it is an objective of Bonniol and his team to aim to link with sentient beings who are sufficiently similar to themselves. In fact, Aerans and humans we now know, share important characteristics that include spirituality, philosophy, humour, music, poetry, awareness of beauty, travel, and appreciation of and assistance from animals—all these characteristics are shared by Aerans and humans. These shared qualities have been well discussed. We have spoken a little about principles and had briefly mentioned Moses receiving 'The Commandments' and Bonniol indicated 'loving their neighbour' to be *their* prime spiritual concept. Regarding travel, he suggested that our vehicular exploration of the solar system would be scarcely worthwhile, since it would merely inform on the nearby *material* and *least interesting* aspect of that part of creation. On the evening of 12th September 2005, I had somehow managed to get us onto the more difficult subjects of 'Big Bang' and 'red-shift'. Bonniol, who had by now become a most treasured friend, responded:

~ "Yes, we have also observed that the bodies in the universe appear to be moving away and this would *imply* expansion, yes. We feel that there is also contraction. But the evidence for contraction is less available. But at this point (in time), it appears that everything is expanding outwards, does it not?"

112

Wonderful! Right away, he refers to both expansion and contraction! But it currently *appears to us* that expansion is winning, or it is the more obvious—and he is being careful not to lead us into knowledge that it is our job to eventually discover for ourselves!

This was all wildly exciting and as the exchange continued, I was saying:

"What we call 'red shift', and various other factors *seem* to indicate, that it is expanding at the present time."

And Graham had added that scientists are of the opinion that it is accelerating in its expansion at the moment:

~ "We also have noticed this yes—that it *appears* to be expanding ever more quickly. So this is a very deep subject, is it not?"

There was without doubt our general agreement to that! And Bonniol then asked the searching question:

~ "Where is it going?"

I briefly recounted the proposition put to Salumet about neither a singularity nor spirit having space or time, to which our teacher had agreed:

~ "So you are of the opinion that this movement in the universe, is not purely physical—that somehow it could be linked to more spiritual dimensions, which allows for the limitlessness of it?"

I attempted to clarify, saying that the start point would be a singularity if we were thinking physically, but the alternative view is simply that all has been created from spirit:

~ **"I think this has to come into the equation yes, when you observe physical things, behaving in ways which appear to be limitless, then you have to begin to think it is tied into its spiritual nature."**

I replied: "So I'm really putting the idea that our scientists are in error, for thinking this through, in entirely physical terms—it doesn't work like that."

~ **"You will never understand it, if you think only physically. When you have spiritual knowledge, then all becomes possible. It would seem that the physical universe, has been endowed with spiritual attributes, which allow it to have unlimited possibilities."**

Graham commented: "That's a nice way of wording it."

Some of us might prefer to see it as a *belt and braces* situation! But I agreed, adding that it is a difficult area for us to think through, whereupon Bonniol responded:

~ **"We are living on little planets, which have been designed with simple rules, but the universe and even the planets as well, are actually outside of those physical rules. In fact we all are outside of the physical rules, once we begin to consider spirit and the interconnectedness of all things."**

I concluded: "Yes I think we have to see it as the physical and the spiritual, being all entwined. They are all much together and yet we can think and perceive entirely physically and we can operate also, at an entirely spiritual level. And in Mind Projection, we are operating at a spiritual level and just making the physical connection. Would that be a reasonable way of putting it?"

~ **"Yes, I can see that you have thought long and hard about these things."**

And I had added: "Yes, and because it operates at a spiritual level, space and time do not come into it and therefore there are no time delays in our dialogue. All is instantaneous."

~ **"Yes we have another example of—we are physical beings and yet, we are able to bypass all these physical laws are we not? And this is another example of how we cannot explain using physical laws, because we are spiritual and so these limits do not apply."**

And finally I was saying: "Yes, so although my initial question seemed rather obscure, it's brought us right back to, I think, a better understanding of Mind Projection work, in the end."

~ **"Yes, I think it's a very good idea to explore all these things around us and the Universe, with all the stars and planets. Space, is a wonderful example is it not, of the limitlessness of the *true* nature of life. It's staring at us all the time, this limitlessness."**

During Bonniol's visit of 19th December 2005, he declared that although he himself had knowledge of NASA's moon mission, he was puzzled—because he could find nothing in Paul's memory banks about Earth's aura. Our planetary aura should have been clearly visible from an approaching or a receding spaceship. This absence of any memory of it he found difficult to understand, and therefore surmised that the information was being withheld from us. [Well, it had already been mentioned by Salumet that facts from that mission were being withheld! And now Bonniol was saying the same thing!] On 8th May 2006, Bonniol confirmed for us that the crop circles appearing on Earth are indeed made by visiting UFOs; adding that these would sometimes be hard for us to see due to the composition of the UFO craft, which can be altered. He also stated that their home planet would be visible in our night sky; so in relative terms they are our near neighbours.

On 10th July 2006 I was able to mention the Russian work with their modern glass-fibre pyramids, and to inquire if Aerans had carried out similar studies of pyramid shape and the energy they produce:

~ "Yes, this is another subject which—crosses the planetary divide if you like. We also have found this benefits our—the energies that we wish to expand or use, can be helped by this shape—this structure."

Very interesting! And Sarah was quick to ask if they also have *ancient* pyramids on their planet:

~ "We do not have ancient pyramids like the ones you have, because our *ancient* ones were not built to last."

We outlined a few facts—the value of seed storage and the accelerated healing of burns:

116

~ "Yes—and now you should be able to understand a little more perhaps, why these shapes have these effects on things."

Well perhaps that is a matter that we should ponder, but Sarah went on to ask about *their* use of pyramids today:

~ "The pyramid shape is very much a part of our structure system, yes."

So Lilian wished to know if their houses include that shape. But it seems that they prefer houses to be on a round base and to have conical form. [There is similarity of form here to the approximately conical shape of the tepee of North American Indians.] It seems that on Aerah, hospitals are round and it is felt that round-form presents a better *living* space. But other shapes are used, each for a specific purpose. I asked about pyramid orientation in respect of planetary spin:

~ "They *must* be orientated—um—to—yes, receive the flow of energy through their *flat* sides."

Q: "Right! So the build-up of energy really depends on the rotation of the planet?"

~ "Yes. That is the main consideration—the way your energies flow. And the pyramid will then harness them better."

It was so splendid to have these facts confirmed and to know that others in the universe find them to be of such value. Bonniol went on to explain that Aerans also use other building shapes—the pentagon as an in-between shape that is favoured for their public buildings. Rod had then voiced his thought that the pyramid shape would make a wonderful burns-healing hospital unit:

~ **"Yes it is a pity is it not, that this knowledge was forgotten?"**

There followed a general response of "Yes!" to this from all present. So I therefore concluded that the pyramid shape should be particularly useful as a place of healing, of storage and of conditioning for things, and asked if that was the same for Aerans:

~ **"Yes, we are able to use this shape in various ways and you will find that although the pyramid shape is useful, it also has some disadvantages too. But it is mainly the energy that is gathered in the shape—that is the important thing."**

We observed that one could sit within the pyramid shape to enhance meditation, but that same shape might be rather awkward as living space:

~ **"—as a meditation site, the pyramid will allow your thoughts to move out of the Earthly realm more easily."**

The following week our conversation on building shape continued. It seems that Aeran homes are conical, and their rising to a point means good energy enhancement. Sleeping quarters are at ground level—they like to be close to the planetary surface when sleeping. There would be a meditation area near the top; and they like to have plenty of oval-shaped windows in their homes.

Bonniol has since (13ᵗʰ November 2006) commented further concerning the visitors to our planet:

~ "You have, I'm sure, had many visitors and you will have more. You are in a time of *denial*—I think that is the word. You have had visitors from other planets—yes. Perhaps the time will come when much more is available. Your world is still denying too much, but you've been told this will change, and you all here have open minds."

Well said! Our friend is perhaps remarkably aux fait with what goes on around our planet and in our skies. (We have since learned that he is able to be *around* without séance group connection, and in some respects knows rather more about us than *we* do!) He is clearly aware, for example, of the official denial of pyramid energies and of the visits from others. And that seems fitting conclusion to Bonniol's input concerning pyramids; also their energy, Aeran building shapes in general and how our planet is being visited by a number of sentient beings. These beings are of far greater intelligence than humans. They are generally well disposed towards us and wish to communicate. It is a fair logical deduction that beings that are progressed sufficiently to have mastered space-travel will have advanced well beyond the naive Earthly belligerency that we must admit to with shame. Space-travel involves what might be termed 'spiritual science' which can only develop once spirit and spirituality have been acknowledged. That in my view gives them a status to be admired and not feared.

A few years later, when our friend was with us on 25th March 2013, we returned to recap on what Bonniol could tell us about pyramids, and I was saying:
"We are beginning to realize now, that when other visitors have been here, the first thing they have done is build a pyramid—to capture or create the energy for their wellbeing while they're here and to provide power for their return journey. I don't know how widespread in the universe pyramid-building is, but it seems to have been a favourite thing to construct pyramids in the past on our planet Earth."

~ "Yes, it is—um—certainly not something that is unique to Earth. We also have pyramids on our planet, which are used to gather the energy. We have—um—developed—um— there is um—we have—"

There can occasionally be a little difficulty with word flow in these exchanges, not that it matters—we are of course so very thankful to have the valuable link across the many light-years of universe, which provides us with so many cross-referenced facts.

~ "The shape of the pyramid is of course a perfect shape for collecting and steering or pointing this particular energy in the direction and when we are sitting inside the pyramids— it can be of great help to use this to focus.

Q: "Yes, would you describe this as an aid to help meditation?"

~ **"The meditation comes from within the person I would say, but the pyramid shape helps to build the power that is generated."**

Sarah asked if the Aeran pyramids were built like ours:

~ **"Yes, the rocks of the earth, we find are the best for *capturing* if you like, the energy—um—the shape itself is important. The position has to be at the right angle for intercepting the flow of energy that is being collected."**

I pointed out that we now know that if we store seeds within the pyramid energy they produce more in the way of crops:

~ **"Yes, they have been used to help with the storing and protection of seeds."**

Q: "Do you use pyramid-storage to assist your agriculture on your planet?"

~ **"We have experimented with this. We find we do not actually need to use them in that way—the seed can be stored in other ways but the pyramids can be used to improve areas which—um—which have conditions which cause problems for plants."**

Q: "Of course, the area around—surrounding pyramids is influenced by the energy, I believe?"

~ "Yes, and if they are located in the right places, this can improve the fertility, if you like, of the area. I would say that is our main interest. We are people who spend a great deal of time working with nature; and where pyramids are used it is usually with—um—in connection to improving the nature in some way—whether it's for our crops—"

Lilian wished to know if pyramids are common to other planets of Bonniol's acquaintance:

~ "Yes, they are a shape—a structure which has a definite affect on the energy flows, and so they can be of use for that."

Rod asked if height to base ratios were all much the same:

~ "I would say the size is not as important. It's the positioning and what they are built with. The size of them varies, depending on the nature of the area and the requirements of the area."

Lilian wanted to know if they are deliberately placed on the ley lines:

~ "Yes, they are used, *always* with the energy lines, yes."

Yes, Earth energy would appear to be very much involved, so that positioning on the ley lines would be an important factor in maximising the energy produced. Mark asked if they are used for healing and purification:

~ "They can certainly be used for healing, yes. And, when you say purification—um—"

Q: "You can purify water, and give it healing quality?"

~ "I would say in the sense that the water would be energised, it would be—um—improved in that way."

I then mentioned about water failing to freeze:

~ "Yes, I would imagine that is due to the greater energy in the water."

Salumet had been quietly working with Eileen up to this point in the proceedings. His work was now complete so that Eileen's consciousness returned and she was now free to place a question. She wished to know, with Bonniol's people being so much more advanced, could they not mind-transmute energy instead of using pyramids for this purpose?

~ "There is—um—we have abilities to transmute energy, yes. The pyramids are permanent features, which require no additional thought or attention. So, in areas where we may wish for nature to create—um—a different energy situation—where plants and nature can begin to grow and benefit from more constant environment—"

I suggested we can think of a pyramid as an ongoing, permanent energy trans-muter that doesn't have to be fed or up-kept in any way:

~ "Yes, we could of course still grow our crops but we feel they are a natural—um—*tool* to use, much like other tools for growing crops."

Q: "Do they alter your climate at all? Do they have any effect on climate?"

~ "Yes, they affect the area around them, and yes, they will have an influence on the climate."

At this point, another began speaking with quite a throaty voice via Jan, from across the room which quite took us by surprise:

~ *"They are regulators! They act as regulators! The weather—it is much more regulated, because of the energy that it transmutes."*

Then addressing Bonniol: ~ *"May I help you sir?"*

Bonniol: ~ "Yes please!"

~ *"You are struggling with language are you not?"*

Well, there had indeed been quite a few 'ums' and pauses in our dialogue this time:

~ "It is sometimes difficult."

~ *"Of course it is! We understand entirely. You are doing magnificently well!"*

There followed a short pause—this was a spirit helper who now spoke via Jan and he continued:

~ *"The older the base of the pyramid that you speak of, it will hold the greater amount of energy—the greater the amount of energy, that will be released from the top."*

Mark: "So they use older materials for the base—"

~ *"Older rocks—yes—the OLDER the Pyramid, the greater is the energy released. So hence, when they are growing their crops, the older energies are the ones that regenerate quicker, better—so their crops are grown nearer to those energies. And the younger crop does not need it quite so much.* **Do you understand?"**

George: "So the longer the pyramid has been there, the better will be the crops."

~ *"Yes! So the older the pyramid base—that's what holds the energy of that plant completely. That's the energy that that plant came from."*

More was said, the spirit helper was thanked for his input and then Lilian was saying: "Are you still there Bonniol?"

~ **"I—I've been having a little break! It is most welcomed, to have someone more familiar with the words to help explain!"**

Jan was then back with us and asked Bonniol if the one who had been with her had explained it well:

~ **"I think there was some information about how the plants grow around the pyramid base—I—"**

I added: **"And how the older the pyramid, the more effective it is."**

On reflection, this was one of our more confusing evenings, but nevertheless usefully informative—and still not quite finished. As Jan fully came to, she was able to describe what she had seen clairvoyantly—seven straight rows of pyramids of different sizes. The larger plants were growing near the largest, and younger plants were near the smaller ones. So this time we had our dear friend Bonniol with us plus one eagerly helping from spirit, plus Jan's clairvoyant picture. What an evening this had turned out to be!

CHAPTER 10 – PYRAMID ENERGY CONFIRMATIONS: SPIRIT REALMS

O n the evening of 20th August 2012 and following a grand session with Salumet, one addressed us via Sarah to say:

~ *"You have shown much interest in the last few sessions about pyramids and I would just like to tell you that I was one of those who was working with the pyramids at that time."*

Well, I think it would be a gross understatement to say we were flabbergasted and could barely believe our good fortune. Here we had an actual *pyramid worker* from the distant past!—a human whom we were able to address as 'Theodore'—one of the Earth who had actually worked with extraterrestrial visitors to help build a pyramid here on Earth! As the conversation progressed, it quickly became evident that Theodore's location was South America, and most likely Cahuachi in the Nazca river valley. I had asked if humans and ETs were learning from each other, and he felt that humans were learning rather more from the ETs than vice versa. Well that figures! The much fuller dialogue concerning all this is presented in our previous book: Earth's Cosmic Ascendancy[1]. It seems that the famous large animal designs of that area depict animals living on the ET's planet—that of course explains why they appear of somewhat strange form to the human way of thinking. Our friend knew the visitors simply as 'the Greens', on account of their greenish tinge, and he and his colleagues knew their planet as the 'Green Planet'. But when Theodore came to *describe* the visitors and the way they travel in groups of fifty; that rang a bell, and with further questioning it became evident that they that they had they also visited the Nevada Desert area, and their humanoid images (displaying 3-fingered hands and extra-wide heads) and details of their living have been inscribed on the Atlatl Rock in the Valley of Fire for any who may care to visit that area to see. We know these delightful beings as 'Crogarians' from their planet known to them as 'Crogaria'. Full details of our group's earlier exchange with them during mind-linked séance and how that came about, are presented in our book: The Chronicles of Aerah – Mind-link Communications across the Universe[2]. Rod asked if the ETs designed and oversaw while humans to do all the hard graft:

~ *"They would never let people do all the hard work. They made our lives so easy. They were able to do so many things that we could not, and we tried very hard to learn from them; and it was hoped that what we learnt we would be able to pass on. But I can see, from life today on this planet, we did not do a very good job in passing this information on."*

Well sadly, that is the way it seems to have turned out. Our friend went on to say that all heavy work need not be heavy. We suggested that such work would have involved dematerialization and power-of-thought and Theodore confirmed this to be so. Paul inquired if he had managed to gain some ability for himself in moving the heavy rocks:

~ *"I was able to do some, but it was not normally by myself—it would take a group of us Earth people together to be able to do what one extraterrestrial could do."*

We could well understand that! And he then went on to describe the procedure as:

~ *"... Putting yourself into a mindset where you are actually being helped to do it. So you would wish for something to happen, and then put yourself into that—I would not say meditation—but getting towards that way where you are not quite in your body and not quite out of it."*

Sara had suggested this might be called: light trance—

~ *"Yes, perhaps you could say that. And it is at this point that you can then begin to work with the—whatever it is you wish to do. So yes, you do not need to concentrate too*

129

hard, but you do need to get yourself away from total Earth thinking."

As regards the pyramid energy, we were assured that the humans of that time and that place were well aware of it, and the Greens needed that additional energy to enable their spaceship to escape Earth's gravity for their return journey. Our quite lengthy dialogue with this *human* pyramid builder who now continues his progress in spirit, confirms the following facts:

➤ Both humans and ETs were well versed in spirituality; they co-operated well and they learned from each other.

➤ Humans were aware of the pyramid energy and all— humans and ETs—benefitted from it.

➤ The energy was needed for spaceship launch, without which the visitors would not be able to return to their home planet. Without that energy, they would be permanently stuck here on Earth.

➤ It follows that the first objective of visitors to Earth, who have a space-ship, will be to build a pyramid—this to provide their various energy requirements.

➤ We all felt so very privileged to have been in receipt of such information from an actual pyramid worker—little dreaming that still more information was to come our way!

It happened just three weeks later (10th September 2012)— our numbers were up with a further three sitting in who had travelled 200 miles from Norfolk to be with us. And I am very happy to be able to report that we all thoroughly enjoyed a truly spectacular evening on that occasion. Following a quite lengthy session with Salumet, we were joined by *another pyramid worker* from spirit! This time, we received valuable data from one living *in the spirit realms* associated with a planet known to its people as 'Simkah'. And it was pure joy for us to discover that these sentient beings from Simkah were the originators of the Bosnian pyramids that two of our team had visited earlier in the year.

This one quickly explained that those involved in the visit of three weeks earlier had prompted this further communication. They are all very happy that we are so interested and that we are beginning to understand and appreciate the nature of interplanetary visits. This new friend went on to confirm that the energy generated was not only for spaceship launch but was also needed for the wellbeing of those from Simkah whilst here. I had been apologetic to our visitor for Earth's slowness to catch on to the tremendous value of, and for our slowness to successfully practice the use of, mind-link communication. But we learned from this one that Earth is not the *only* planet in the universe to be a bit backward in this respect. We *are indeed* backward, but this visitor was certainly not eager to put us down. He was nicely inspiring, taking care not to discourage us in any way— genteel one might say! Paul indicated that we would be delighted if they decided to return to Earth and build pyramids again:

~ *"Well, maybe we can arrange something—"*

Well, of course, that would be just grand! But our new friend pointed out a problem—Earth has changed, and there are now so few places on this planet where they would be left alone to do all that they would need to do. And we understand they would still need to build a pyramid, but perhaps it could be a little smaller than before. Interruption mid-session could easily mean being trapped here on Earth permanently. Ray, one of our visitors, had asked an intriguing question: "How long would it take to build one?" And the answer was in effect: it takes as long as it takes! Well, such a project *could* be fairly instantaneous, but the time element would depend very much on the people working with them, and I guess that means their spiritual abilities. There was more said on pyramid size, and it was pointed out to us that our computers have come down in size remarkably from how they used to be. What a good example! And it does again serve to illustrate that some in spirit keenly follow our progress here on Earth. Some of those in spirit know as much about ourselves as *we* do and perhaps understand us rather more! He then went on to say that we should not push the idea of a further visit *completely* away because they are just as keen as we are. It could actually happen!—if it was felt that it would be of benefit to our planet at this time.

132

Paul had questioned the size of Simkahns—they are a little shorter than humans, we understand. That makes perfect sense because, when walking the Bosnian pyramid tunnels humans have to stoop a little in places. Olive had asked about mode of communication and was assured that the speaker could relay messages to and from others in spirit and to physical beings living planetary lives. He added: 35,000 years ago (*his* figure for Bosnian pyramid age) planetary lives and abilities were a little different!—a thought not to be lightly brushed aside. The 8-ton ceramic artefact that resides in one Bosnian pyramid tunnel was discussed and it was confirmed that this was a self-regenerating potable water supply—this filled automatically with water without wetting the tunnel floor. Pyramid construction was a combined operation involving both the visitors and humans. It was very clearly stated that ET-constructions were mind-created in situ while human-made units were constructed elsewhere and levitated into position. All was clearly very well planned and overseen indeed and demonstrates an admirably superior intelligence. As this conversation came to an end, much gratitude and good feelings were expressed by all. Someone declared: "You must come again!" to which our visitor had replied:

~ *"Yes, I am beginning to smile because maybe I come again—for real!"*

As reported here, this exchange is very much condensed. It is reported in full in our earlier publication[1]. And so as aether sweeps past the ancient well-constructed pyramids, energy is produced. This is confirmed by sentient beings living on other planets, by those now in spirit and by modern Earthly laboratories.

PART 4 – AETHER DYNAMICS

CHAPTER 11 – ENDLESS MOVEMENTS

Mainstream scientists of the West have ignored aether existence throughout the 20th century, following what was most probably a misinterpretation at the time of the Michelson-Morley experiment. And even today there may be laughter if I dare to mention that word 'aether' in their presence in anything like serious context; a favourite follow-up remark being: But you cannot show me a reference to that in a peer-reviewed journal! Perfectly correct! But the problem where aether is concerned is that journal editors and reviewing peers are so often peering in the wrong direction. Not all of the work revealing significant facts gets into peer-reviewed journals these days! And in order to acknowledge the work of Russian astrophysicist Dr Nikolai Kozyrev (1908-1983), it would have been necessary for those in the West to take seriously the scientific work of Eastern Bloc scientists during the Cold War period, and that did not officially come to an end until 1991. So, it is small wonder that the work of this genius continues to be virtually unknown in the West!

Kozyrev had displayed brilliance from a very early age, publishing his first paper at seventeen. He then rapidly became a distinguished astronomer and teacher. But sadly, in 1937, during Josef Stalin's repressive period, he was sent to a concentration camp for eleven horrific years. Politics can get in the way of real progress in so many different ways! But Kozyrev retained his brilliance of mind regardless of the politics and continued to think things through—the predominance of spiral form in the universe and the structures within the universe. And it was a blessing that, on his release in 1948 he was ready to continue working with a renewed vigour.

Meanwhile, there are two scientists, each having the name: Dr Harold Puthoff in the West—one in America, known for his work in the field of remote viewing and other pursuits, and one at Cambridge University, UK. The latter is to be remembered for his exemplary work of searching for *energy in a vacuum.* He took careful measures to shield an evacuated chamber from any possible radiations, and cooled it to absolute zero (-273^0 C). Then following various tests, he found he was obliged to describe his chamber as a 'seething cauldron of energy', which he called 'zero-point energy', and the zone he called a 'zero-point field'. Photons and various particles seemed to be appearing from nowhere for millionths of a second, then vanishing again—returning to the zero-point field. These were termed 'virtual particles' and the zero-point field has been described as 'a quantum foam of virtual particles and photons'. Well perhaps language begins to fail us here. But one reason for this is it has become a firm fashion in the West to not mention that word 'aether'. Mention the out-of-favour word 'aether' and there is a very strong chance indeed that your paper will be excluded from peer-reviewed journals—that also would likely mean loss of any research funding. So there are papers that use terms such as 'zero point field', 'zero point energy', 'dark matter', 'dark energy', 'vacuum flux', 'virtual particles', 'quantum medium' and more recently, following the CERN large hadron collider project, 'the Higgs Ocean'—home to the Higgs Bosun. [Official recognition of aether per se would of course herald a final death blow to Big Bang theory and projects connected!] But atoms and molecules require energy from somewhere in order that they maintain their status quo and that energy comes from the zero-point field alias aether. Puthoff used a candle analogy to help explain, in which the wax of the candle provides the energy to maintain its flame.

Perhaps we should also mention Thomas Bearden's observation that the four light propagation equations of James Clerk Maxwell are a reduced form of the original set of equations; this in order to simplify calculations. In reduced form, they describe light as a purely electromagnetic waveform with electric and magnetic vectors, each perpendicular to the direction of travel. But the set of equations in their original rather more extended form say rather more—they take into account the longitudinal energy propagation, much more akin of course to sound wave propagation.

So, having given mention to timely parallel key developments in the West, let us now return again to the East and to the work of Nikolai Kozyrev during those Cold War years. And needless to say, the Cold War years are to be much regretted for a number of reasons. He also has used a simplifying analogy to explain the basis of *his* experiments. Kozyrev likened all physical objects in the sea of aether to well-soaked sponges immersed in water. The aether impregnates all, and the sponges can be operated upon physically—by spinning, heating, deformation etc—to make them hold just a little more or a little less water. In the aether environment, weight changes of objects due to spinning, heating, deforming or breaking would be extremely minute, so a central aspect of his work was to construct highly sensitive weight-measuring devices. Another aspect of his work has been to devise subtle physical ways of acting upon his test objects. And a strong influence in this work has been the knowledge that this part of our galaxy is subject to right-handed spin vortices within its aether. Perhaps we should also bear in mind that there have been thousands of follow-up experiments to Kozyrev's work, with publication in peer-reviewed journals of the East.

Theory has it that spinning 'torsion' fields are of two kinds— static and dynamic. Natural objects, flowers for example, have their static torsion fields that are sometimes referred to as their 'aura', and such static fields or auras can be rendered clearly visible by means of, for example, Kirlian photography. And auras will be visible to a greater or lesser extent to those with developed psychic abilities. The static torsion fields—auras—do not radiate energy from themselves, but rotating sources such as the sun and Earth in orbit, result in dynamic torsions. Such travelling torsion waves provide a basis for one explanation of gravity. Within the aether, gravity and spin would appear to have just as much a paired relationship as electric and magnetic—a profound thought! Kozyrev was able to demonstrate that rigid objects in an aether flow, exhibit small weight changes while flexible objects exhibit changes in their elasticity or viscosity. [And we have also noted in chapter 8 that pyramid energy significantly reduces oil viscosity in nearby oil fields.] He has also shown that torsion fields can be absorbed by sugar. Now this may at first seem very odd indeed, but we should not overlook a fact that is well-known in organic chemistry: that sugars can be dextro- or laevo-rotatory—that is, their solutions can rotate the plane of polarized light in either of two twisting directions; some sugars one way and some the opposite way, according to their molecular configuration. So there could well be a subtle connection here, between torsion field and the chemistry of certain optically active organic compounds. And Kozyrev has shown that aluminium can shield physical matter from the effect of torsion waves and mirrors can reflect.

139

On what principles were his mechanical detection and measuring equipment based? His devices were not static. They were based on rotating gyroscopes or an asymmetric swinging pendulum. The underlying principle seems to be that things in motion are much more sensitive than devices that are stationary. And it is interesting that the direction of the detector's movement can be extremely important. He found that a vibrating gyroscope or one that was conducting electricity exhibited weight loss if rotating counter-clockwise. But no weight loss resulted from clockwise rotation, suggesting that the spinning torsion field of Earth's gravity may have been revealed. The spin orientation of a gyroscope may well relate to the 'Coriolis Effect', which in turn relates to Earth rotation.

Gustave-Gaspard Coriolis gave his name in 1835 to the mysterious rotational motion that influences Earth's weather patterns. It is a counter-clockwise movement in Northern Hemisphere and a clockwise movement in Southern Hemisphere. As a scientific fact, this rotational effect remains unknown to many, but it is sufficiently real to be an acknowledged major influence on our weather systems and the military have to make allowance for it when firing long range artillery—or they miss target! It seems fairly clear that the rotation is a torsion (twisting) of the aether that arises from planetary rotation. In Japan, G. Hayasaka and S. Tekeyuchi found that a counter-clockwise rotating gyroscope falls more slowly than would be expected, but not so if it spins the other way. Their work confirms that of Kozyrev—and both sets of experiments were of course conducted in the Northern Hemisphere. So the Coriolis Effect is an excellent demonstration of aether dynamics, as revealed by falling gyroscopes.

Dr Harold Aspden of Cambridge University, UK, has also worked with gyroscopes and given his name to the 'Aspden Effect'. The central wheel of his gyroscope was a powerful magnet. He applied energy of 1,000 joules to achieve a maximum rotation speed. After it had stopped rotating, he let it stand for one minute before re-starting. But this time it required only 100 joules to power the gyroscope to the same maximum speed. Surprising perhaps as well as interesting! Why so? The likely explanation is that magnet plus aether were rotated the first time. When the magnet stopped, the aether continued its rotation, so that much less energy was required to achieve maximum speed the second time, when only the magnetic wheel consumed it. So we can see this as an interesting experimental result that can readily be explained through the recognition of aether dynamics.

It seems that electrostatic and electromagnetic fields always have in association, a torsion component. It has been shown that this has to be so. A permanent magnet has a right-handed torsion field extending from its north polarity end and a left-handed torsion field extending from its south polarity end. I expect we are all familiar with the way iron filings on a sheet of paper can reveal the magnetic force lines from a magnet placed beneath the paper, and how those force lines from the poles curl around and form loops. Although a common metallic element, iron is special in that its atom has four unpaired electrons. A travelling unpaired electron is in effect an electric current with an associated magnetic field. And a permanent magnet can be made by acting on the crystal 'domains' of the metal that contain these electrons, so that the many domains align, and each 'mini-magnet' reinforces another. That is what makes a permanent magnet; and we should not overlook the fact that we have also at the same time made a torsion field with a right-handed and a left-handed emergence. Our planet is likewise, on account of its iron core and its rotation. The rotating iron core produces a magnetic field. So our planet has its magnetic field that directs a compass needle; also of course, it is accompanied by a torsion field.

A very important observation to be made in all this is that Kozyrev has conducted experiments at various locations and has found location to be a significant factor in the results obtained. His most striking results were obtained in the extreme North, within 5^0 45' of the North Pole. So more torsion wave energy flows into the Earth in this Polar region; while there is a less marked flow for locations closer to the equator (these observed effects being analogous to the torsion field of a bar magnet). Whilst on the subject of magnets and their associated torsion fields we might also mention the so-called 'magnetization of water' phenomenon. Experiments have been conducted in which the form of crystallization of distilled water has been influenced by the presence of bar magnets. It is reasoned that the influence on crystallisation is due to, not the magnetic field as such, but the associated torsion field of the magnet.

Many of the original Kozyrev experiments have since been repeated and sometimes extended by others and his results have received confirmation. The data obtained all points to a dynamic aether such that the various movements within it can be revealed—by experiments that have been conducted with extreme care. Kozyrev's work, considered in relation to that of others appears to account for or to explain several known facts that have appeared curious, such as the Coriolis Effect, the Aspden Effect and the so-called magnetization of water phenomenon. This all adds up to a very strong case for the existence of torsion effects and flow patterns within the aether, so that we may view the medium as truly dynamic. But if this is so, then surely there is an inconsistency here with the constancy of the speed of light? Maxwell's equations and Einstein's $E = mc^2$ would appear to relate to light having a fixed velocity, and this has been very precisely measured as 299,792,458 metres/sec. But if light travels through a *shifting* aether, is this just a mean value for c as seen from Earth? One can readily accept a fixed c referenced to aether per se, but if the aether has movement within itself, then light would surely sometimes travel a little faster and sometimes a little more slowly, in accord with its movement—as referenced to Earth? Well, it is interesting that this status quo was suspected by Bryan Wallace through the 1960s. An experiment that *he* conducted involved a set of high-power radio transmitters arranged across the US to obtain data in relation to this, and he noticed that certain radar measurements within the solar system failed to confirm constancy for c. Space satellites launched in 1972 and1973 have also provided further data which has anomalies. So there might possibly be grounds for supposing that aether dynamics cause some small variations in light speed as seen from Earth. Quite early on in Salumet's visits (1st August 1994), I had in fact asked about the speed of light being a limiting factor for us here on Earth in our gaining knowledge of the universe:

~ **"Yes. Let me say you are indeed limited by what you know and understand. There are other galaxies—let me say this to you: how do you suppose there are space travellers, if they do not travel quicker than the speed of light, as *you* know it? That must answer your question simply and straightforwardly. *The speed of light* is only the Earth's conception of speed. There are many things, which the Earth is not aware of, as such, but you will become more and more knowledgeable in these matters, as time progresses."**

How very true! The question was answered in such a way that we were sufficiently able to understand at that time; and following many years of Salumet's further teaching, we have indeed since become more knowledgeable, and are now beginning to question, not only the aether and its movements, but that well established pillar of mainstream science—light speed. We now know that there are several ways in which *the Earth's conception of the speed of light* can be exceeded. One of those ways we now know to be *wormhole travel.* But in the context of astronomy, what is a wormhole? Before answering this question, it would be as well that we first examine the nature of black holes.

CHAPTER 12 – BLACK HOLES

A recently introduced term that has found use in the scientific reasoning is 'Process Physics'. This addresses a move away from that rigidly fixed four-dimensional space-time model of the universe that was embarked upon following relativity—and the imagined warping of a space-time grid to illustrate the effect of gravity. That had been Einstein's clever invention to suit the limited data available at that time. But now, Process Physics is described as a *dynamic model* in which 'space and quantum matter' emerge from a system that is essentially 'self-organizing'. And what is described as 'space and quantum matter' is of course aether—such expression for what precedes the formation of matter is acceptable as current scientific mainstream jargon, just so long as the actual term 'aether' does not get used! That remains unacceptable to mainstream science, and the use of new terminology is always suggestive of actual progress rather than reversion to old ways of thinking! But if process physics finds acceptance in some circles at least, and presents a *dynamic model* for the aether; also sees that dynamic model as *self-organizing*, then this has to be seen as a useful step forward.

Whilst Einstein's actual equations and mathematics are not presented here, it is nevertheless appropriate that we continue to acknowledge his genius, and to observe that the set of ten *field equations* of general relativity have since resulted in some further valuable steps forward. In 1915, Einstein published data on the interaction of his 'curved space-time', 'mass' and 'gravity' leading to a tensor (set of vector components) equation providing a description of space-time geometry. Accompanied by a necessary making of certain assumptions, exact solutions to the field equations demonstrate possibilities of gravitational phenomena, including the 'rotating black hole'. So the set of mathematical equations actually postulate the existence of black holes. So what is a black hole? Is it simply a structure derived from general relativity as no more than just a mathematical possibility? In its simplest *physical* description, it is a body with extremely powerful gravity—so powerful that absolutely nothing, not even light, can escape from it. Is this a reality or is it only an on-paper extreme case? It is both. It derives from the Field Equations, but black holes are now known to actually have their place in the universe. There is now evidence for their existence. And if such powerful gravity can prevent light from escaping then we might argue that light and gravity must be connected in some way.

It is reasoned that a black hole has a theoretical shell of influence, beyond which light cannot escape. This shell has been given the name 'event horizon'. Once light reaches the event horizon it cannot escape the black hole interior. The black hole that has been reasoned theoretically is a mathematical entity having no mass evaluation as such; and following the null interpretation of the Michelson-Morley experiment, space in 1915 was of course seen as a vacuum. It followed at that time therefore, that regardless of how much light is absorbed, no mass-change could take place as a result. So how should we now, in the present, regard a black hole in physical terms? The view of scientific mainstream is that a black hole forms as the result of a star collapsing, having exhausted its nuclear fuel in the production of heat and light. In this situation there is no more heat being produced so that atoms move closer together—the star collapses and becomes extremely dense. And that density equates to extreme gravity. That seems to be the mainstream thinking. But it is now known that there are what are termed 'super-massive black holes' at the centres of galaxies, and of course, there has to be good reason for this—which star-collapse fails to explain.

Leslie had queried the nature of black holes with Salumet as early as 3rd April 1995. There had been prior word received from one in spirit about their crushing gravitational property and how it would be impossible for any human to survive in one, and it was thought at that time that something that had also been said might indicate that they are gateways from one universe to another. So Leslie sought clarification on these points, to which Salumet had replied:

~ "Let me speak to you on this matter. I would say to you that no one could survive within the pressure—your scientists are correct in that respect."

He then went on to explain that there would be a likely misunderstanding, and following the failure of a being to survive, it would be merely a gateway from the physical existence to spirit world:

~ "These black holes, as you call them—I prefer to say, it is an abundance of energy in a particular spot. It is *not* a gateway to other universes. I have said before, you do not travel between—you are speaking of these energy fields as though it were a physical tunnel. That cannot be."

Leslie had continued: "So scientists are right about there being excessive, undreamed of gravity within?"

~ "It is just so. They have it almost correct, but not quite. I believe I have heard said, that you can be encapsulated within these black holes. Not so, not so. We speak here again on many deep matters—matters I think you would find difficult to understand."

And in 1995 we could readily accept that! As time and teaching moved on, there would be progress and we would be able to enjoy a slightly better understanding. But moving on to 2007, my thoughts on black holes still remained very unclear, and after all, so far as the general scientific thinking in this field was concerned, the subject of black holes was highly conjectural. A question placed to Salumet, I now know contained some error, but my question had included the phrase "...certain structures, like black holes for example, where this universe seems to be disappearing..." My meaning was that light and matter seem to be continually drawn into the black holes; and our teacher had responded:

~ **"Yes, I would encourage that thinking."**

Then, during our 24th September 2012 meeting I sought a little more, and received affirmative responses to the questions: "Spirit has always been?" and "Mind is part of spirit and spirit has a number of parts?" and "What we call 'energetic void' extends throughout the universe?" I had then asked if that 'energetic void' has also always been, or has it emerged as part of creation:

~ **"It is a part of Creation, but it has the ability to change. So yes, it has always been."**

Q: "And I imagine spirit has to be in association *with* the energetic void?"

~ "Yes, you cannot separate the two."

Q: "Going on from there—if the energetic void is part of evolution, then I would imagine that it continues to be created and is in pace in a way, with the expanding Universe?"

~ "Yes, as I have said, it is able to change, and the word 'void' is slightly misleading I feel. What is 'void'?"

Well, I had been using the term 'energetic void' that had become an in-word featured in the material that I had been reading, and I replied that I felt it meant 'no atoms present'.

~ "Yes, but it is still part of all Creation. You cannot dismiss this."

Well, that seems important then, that the so-called energetic void is a part of the ongoing creation. More was said, with Salumet confirming that mind belongs to spirit, and I was advised to keep my thoughts at a simplistic level. Jan pointed out that consciousness is also part of spirit, and it therefore cannot be seen as void.

~ "*All* is energy, whether you give it a name or not. Yes, that is true."

I had then added: "Well the old-fashioned term was 'aether', which is perhaps a better word."

~ "Yes I would agree. I would prefer to use that word. It is basically a spiritual energy, and all is part of creation—you cannot separate it."

I thanked Salumet for his valuable guidance on this and observed that it should help if we use appropriate words for our descriptions.

~ "Yes, it is easy to complicate that which is simple. But it is understandable also."

[Seeking word origin—in Homeric Greece, the word 'aether' was used to describe the pure essence breathed by the gods. And in Plato's 'Timaeus' it is seen as: the most translucent kind of air. Moving on to the 17th/18th century, the Swiss mathematician Johann Bernoulli described space as being permeated by an immense number of minute whirlpools. These he maintained, would confer a perfect elasticity and this permits wave transmission—the aether's luminiferous property. Perfect elasticity results from each whirlpool pressing against its neighbours, and electromagnetic phenomena manifest from this elastic environment. Aether is described as 'a sea of aether whirlpools'. A paper by Frederick Tombe (2006)[3], expands on the notion of a sea of tiny vortices, that leads to an explanation of electromagnetism.]

Our conversation with Salumet continued with Jan adding a kindly word, pointing out how I was versed in science, had an inquisitive scientific mind, and this was helping us in our journey forward. I had replied that I was doing my best to relate all to spirit and to unite scientific thinking with spiritual considerations, whereupon our teacher continued:

~ **"And that is his purpose within this group—each one of you has a place and a purpose."**

Exactly so! Then Salumet referred to his mission to our world, explaining:

~ **"It takes quite a long time to find those people who are suitable, not only in spirit, but in their daily thinking. All are different within this group, and yet you are all as one. Unity has become purer as time has passed by and for this I am eternally grateful."**

An encapsulating statement most elegantly expressed, and we of course also expressed *our* gratitude for the guidance received.

Our meeting of 10th June 2013 was memorable. I had on that occasion desperately wanted to find out more about the energy generated by a pyramid sweeping through the aether and took a bold step. I asked if I might explain to Salumet

how the energy is produced, and perhaps he would tell me if
I am wrong. He had replied:

~ **"I find that amusing!** *You*—**are going to tell** *me*—**about**
*energy***?! My dear friend, I do not often want to smile when
I am with you, but that is a new experience for me!"**

I think this might have been seen by our teacher as *role
reversal*—and as hoots of laughter subsided I presented my
case, whilst admitting to some measure of tongue-in-cheek in
that presentation—which our teacher of course well
understood—I explained:
"We've received information from *so many* different sources
now—from physical beings, from beings in the spirit realms
of other planets and from you. Putting it all together, I think
that the energy is developed through the Earth's rotation and
the surface of the Earth being swept by the aether—and the
well sited pyramid is, through planetary rotation, swept by the
aether. And to use a physical analogy, this *distorts* the aether
in such a way that *Earth energy* is drawn up through the base
of the pyramid and rises. It has been stated that that energy is
'resourceful', and I think this means that it is used to being
connected within the Earth and has association with *ley-
lines*—where pyramid sites are chosen. That energy is rising
and resourceful and goes to beings or things within the
pyramid. It also goes to plants growing in the area around the
pyramid, and to perhaps larger areas where there are groups of

pyramids. So the pyramid energy assists the growth of plants, and it continues rising and is refined as it reaches the apex of the pyramid and produces a beam of refined energy, which can be used to launch a dematerialised spaceship for return journey of the beings who visited our Earth and built the pyramid. I wonder how accurate that description would be, or would you care to comment?"

This was followed by more laughter as Salumet said:

~ **"Well my dear friend that is quite a story! Yes, I understand—I understand your interest, but what you have left out is *cosmic energy*. I say those words again: *Cosmic energy.*"**

Q: "Yes—so would this be energy within the aether?"

~ **"No, this energy goes further than the aether, it is cosmic—it belongs to all of Creation. There are many areas in your world, not only on the sites of pyramids that have great Earth energy. This energy is utilised as you said, by many of the ley-lines which lie within your world. I would say to you: the combination of *Earth, Air, Aether* and *Cosmic Energy*, is where the most powerful energies exist. The energy that brings into your world *alien craft*, as you call them, is utilised by the cosmic energy. I want you to realise the great part that this plays, not only on your planet, but in many others. Without this cosmic energy there would be no space travel—you understand? It is an energy not spoken of, or rarely mentioned. I understand your interest in the pyramids because they can be *seen* by the human eye as great places of energy. But**

155

yes—what you say is mostly correct I would say, but the one missing factor is the *cosmic energy*.”

It was a significant addition to our understanding. I think Salumet was on the whole quite pleased with my little foray, and he suggested that I should visit the *Halls of Learning* when I get to spirit world. I agreed that would be an interesting prospect for when that time comes. Lilian then inquired if the space-travellers might themselves be aware of the cosmic energy:

~ **“They may not be aware, but they know that it can be utilised. They use the energy but they do not always understand it.”**

I added: “Of course the vast majority on this planet do not believe that friends from across the universe have built pyramids here, but I see pyramids as the hardest of hard evidence for their visits.”

~ **“Yes—they are part of their visits, but there is so much in your world that will never fully be understood. It is impossible for you to *fully* understand, until you come to our world and then all becomes much clearer. You understand?”**

That we readily accept, and it is so good that we have unquestionable confirmation from Salumet of such an important fact. Graham added that astronomers are finding it puzzling that the galaxies in our universe don’t seem to have enough matter in them for their contents to be held together by means of the force of gravity. So as a way of explaining this they invent new types of energy which they call *dark matter.*

~"**Yes, because they do not understand what energy exists—what matter exists—it is outside of their own intelligence. Yes, you are quite correct."**

Q: "That is the cosmic energy which you have just mentioned?"

~ **"Yes, yes; so now my dear friends, I feel we have spoken enough for this time."**

Well, to say that we were well pleased with the advance in awareness as the result of this enlightening visit would be gross understatement; and as the session closed, our teacher was duly thanked for the information given, whereupon he responded with:

~ **"Yes, and I have to thank you for the amusement that I have felt and have not experienced before!"**

So this particular meeting ended with further laughter, Sarah adding: "Well I was going to say: I haven't heard you laugh before Salumet, so as we say, there is always a first time for everything!"

And we were left with the thought: Perhaps that further factor—the *cosmic energy*—is what makes the universe self-thinking and so totally connected.

So we are encouraged to go back to the drawing board and to think further regarding disappearance of universe in the vicinity of black holes. It also is becoming clear that there are connections between black holes and galactic centre, aether dynamics, and to that little known and even less contemplated cosmic energy. But there remains the essential purpose within this universe of the black hole. This matter will be dealt with in due course.

CHAPTER 13 – WORMHOLES

In looking to the history of wormholes, we must again turn to a development that has followed on from Einstein's General Theory of Relativity. So much has resulted from Einstein's work! In 1916 Karl Schwarzschild solved Einstein's field equations for non-rotating black holes and Ludwig Flamm suggested the possibility of a link between black holes and a tunnel through space-time that would connect them. Then in 1933 Einstein and Nathan Rosen solved further equations that would lead to recognition of what has been termed the 'Einstein-Rosen Bridge'. And this became the first mathematically constructed—on paper—wormhole, but not at that time named as such. It was seen as a connection that could link different regions of space-time, and this would be consistent with the principle that space is warped by huge mass which can in effect lead to a bridge *through* the space-time to connect galaxies. It was some time later, in 1957, that John Wheeler actually coined the term 'wormhole', this as a conversational term for the Einstein-Rosen Bridge. Then in 1985, it was indicated in a paper by Kip Thorne and colleagues that *traversable wormholes* could indeed conceivably exist. The mouth of such a wormhole was considered to be in the nature of a *rotating black hole*. In fact, in order to be traversable, one end would be a rotating black hole while the other would have to be a 'white hole' to allow exit. A Schwarzschild wormhole would not be seen as traversable—it would be seen merely as, but nevertheless as a very interesting, hypothetical topological feature of the space-time. But a further factor to be addressed is that valid solutions from General Relativity seem to require introduction of 'exotic matter'; that is defined as matter having negative mass—if that is possible. Perhaps it should be born in mind that expressions derived from mathematical equations, offer to the intellect *canonical extreme possibilities* that do not necessarily form part of reality.

Well, perhaps it is interesting that the above listed sequence of details has led to the notion that traversable wormholes that could conceivably be used as short cuts through space-time could conceivably exist—there is a theoretical basis, initially derived *purely* from mathematics, for thinking such a structure to be possible. But of course, it is all still very conjectural and not quite fully understood. It was necessary to introduce the hypothetical exotic matter as a means of keeping wormhole ends open and there has been mention in the literature for wormhole ends to spin at the speed of light in order to achieve this. It all remains so very highly conjectural; nevertheless, with mainstream scientists still maintaining that space is a vacuum, it is really quite astonishing that there should have been any progress at all in this direction! After all, how could a vacuum become configured into a wormhole? How can a vacuum be configured to become *anything* but a vacuum? But there has been considerable intelligent thought given in pursuit of this concept, and there has clearly been an attractive spin-off for the writers of science fiction—they have been quick to latch onto the idea of traversable wormholes through space in the interest of speeding up their storylines. That, I guess had to be a natural outcome! But on reflection, now—in the present—now that we know that wormholes do indeed exist, it is truly amazing and a great credit to theorists that they have come so close to providing an on-paper-proof of wormhole reality. But hey! Wait a minute! How exactly do *we* know that wormholes are a reality? What proof is there of their existence? How do *we* know if the view of scientific mainstream is that they are merely a mathematical conjecture?

Some of the Bonniol visits to us have been, not only valuable, but also wildly beyond our expectation; the visit of 8th May 2006 certainly being no exception. At the outset, we had learned more of our ET friend's abilities—when he is not actually using Paul for speech, he can still be in the room listening to what goes on. There are aspects of, as well as degrees of, communication that we as humans had not for one minute anticipated. On this occasion, Sarah had referred to Earth's ET visitors travelling in space-craft and their attempts to communicate with us via the crop circles. She had inquired if Bonniol can also travel in this way or is he restricted to the mind-link format:

~ "We only travel *great* distances in this way (mind-link). We prefer this way, rather than using our craft to visit other planets. We could visit *some*, but we are not able to visit *all* planets."

Q: "And would these be the same sort of craft as you use to get to your moon?"

~ **"We have a number of different ones, but something similar to that one, yes. Your visitors who make the patterns in your crops—"**

As our friend paused, Lilian had observed that lights are sometimes seen in the sky on these occasions, as opposed to actual craft, and our question was elaborated a little: "But there are connections with what we call UFOs—unidentified flying objects—which are often seen as lights travelling in the sky, and we think the crop circles are a means of communicating, that we haven't entirely fathomed yet."

Sarah then referred back, saying: "You were going to say something, Bonniol?

~ **"I was pondering my words carefully. These ships are often very hard to see, because they are made of different substances and not always physical as such."**

Q: "I believe they can be material form or dematerialised form—"

~ **"But they are there for you to observe and you *will* see more. That is what we understand."**

Our friend from across the universe clearly understands much from his spirit contacts and his various sentient being connections that the majority of humans, with absolute certainty do not!

Graham inquired if they had visited Aerah:

~ "The ones you are observing have never been to our planet. We are—we are—"

Lilian volunteered: "Too far away possibly?"

~ "Yes, that is one issue. Another is: there are certain beings you would find it harder to meet with, for different reasons. Some have such a different energy pattern. It can be difficult to even *notice* them. Some worlds find it easier than others. We have been communicating with your visitors—some of your visitors."

Well! Much seems to be going on out there of which we have been oblivious! There were more questions and interjections, before Bonniol was able to continue with reference to his communications with the circle-makers:

~ "The link is not of the same—it is a link which is still very unclear to *us*."

Richard wished to know if they are from somewhere not too far distant and we understand from our friend that their star is visible in our night sky—a part of our galaxy that features in this region of space.

~ "With the kind of craft that *we* have, we cannot at this time make that journey."

I had then asked: "Would I be right in saying that, using the principle of dematerialisation, one can travel very much faster through space, but even with that procedure, one would still be restricted to travelling within a galaxy?"

~ "It is not so much the ability to hop from one galaxy to another. This is possible through certain—'holes', if you like. But these holes only run from certain places. It is not possible to use them for *every* part—every place—"[2]

Wow! This part of the conversation I think took us all by surprise! It was an amazing revelation and I quickly replied: "This is I think what we call 'wormholes'."

~ "And you need to use them at certain times—yes. They are not always open."

Now clearly this was truly remarkable, and I instantly felt so grateful to those 'wormhole theorists' for equipping us with their conjectural data that enabled us to slot into this Bonniol exchange so neatly! And Sarah wished to know the reason for wormhole closure:

~ "They are governed by certain laws I believe. They are in one direction at certain times, and then they switch. So you have to wait for them to be going in the right way."

Richard suggested: "I would assume the reason for that is part of the universe is shifting, in the same way as our solar system

---

[2] These wormholes in specific locations may explain why it is that certain places on Earth have many sightings of UFOs, such as Area 51, while others do not—it could be that these areas are near to the entry points of the wormholes.

is shifting around the sun. So you could probably plot it by calendar—"

~ "Yes, if you use them much, then you *know* how they operate—you wouldn't need to look at a map—they do follow very precise patterns."

Graham: "Are they very common?"

~ "Yes, there are many of them."

Graham: "So all you have to do is enter one, and you pop out the other end. That's all you have to do, get into it?"

~ "Yes, they are almost instantaneous."

Well, this brings to mind those earlier words of Salumet from 1994, when he said *The speed of light is only the Earth's conception of speed.* Now we understand just a little more.

Sarah: "So you would travel in what form?"

~ "—this would be in your craft. These are for when you are visiting with your *physical* body."

Sarah: "And what is the craft powered by?"

~ "The craft that *we* use, as we have said, are powered by energy from our plants, but other worlds have different forms of energy. We *would* tell you more about your visitors, but there is a certain feeling that it is better to—"

—Make the discoveries for ourselves. That should of course be the way forward for humanity and all other sentient planetary beings—use our consciousness in order to *develop* consciousness. That would appear to be a universal principle. And of course, the various cultures of sentient beings that exist are free to choose the energy source that best suits.

Jan: "So there's a protocol that we need to abide by—"

~ "Yes, we are not supposed to give you *all* the information!"

Within the group, we are all very much aware of the way information has been withheld from public, and I had observed: "Yes I must say, you are more forthcoming than our governments have been!"

Jan went on to explain how our governments are inclined to dismiss the evidence for UFO existence, even when they have been photographed or filmed by many people. She explained that, if UFOs can dematerialise, then the materialist attitude to thinking just cannot accommodate this; so UFOs are officially dismissed as an atmospheric feature, the erroneous presentation of which, although deceitful, in some very minute measure might just be understandable. So governments are trying to say the lights in the sky are atmospheric phenomena and not visiting craft. And so, Jan had then wished to know if Bonniol could understand her contention as to their way of dealing with what was happening:

~ "Yes—yes. This—um—is why this meeting of your visitors, the timing of it is so important. Every step has to be carefully taken—so that everything is ready for that time."

Jan: "Bonniol, with due respect, why would you choose a group such as ourselves—little groups that meet in little rooms like this. Why would you choose to give us the information that you have if we're not actually as a planet ready to accept that? Why give it to us if we can't use that information?"

More was said on this theme, and if governments are in effect unapproachable or not acting in the best interest of the people; then I guess one has to begin somewhere, if communication between the sentient beings of the universe is to go forward at all; and Bonniol's concluding comment following all this was:

~ "Yes I think these preliminary trips, if you like, usually take place with smaller numbers who *are* prepared to listen."

That I believe to be the crux of the matter—the process has to begin somewhere—with groups such as we have, who quite simply *are prepared to listen* and who *are prepared to discuss the pros and cons (if any!)*. When governing bodies and scientific mainstream are either too insensitive or stuck in their ways, then it has initially to be a network of open-minded small groups across the planet. This group, as equally in the case of a number of others, knows about UFOs and crop circles—we understand, apply basic logic and accept. But many—so many people have been so conditioned that acceptance is simply beyond their grasp. They will need more time to adjust.

167

I concluded: "It's very nice for us to have our beliefs confirmed in this way by talking with Bonniol. And with our beliefs being confirmed, we are in a stronger position to talk about this to other people. I think this is an important factor here."

~ **"Yes, and in time you will explore much more fully. And I am sure that will take place at the right time, whenever that time happens to be."**

Lilian: "So it's got to be the right time—"

~ **"Yes."**

And finally, Sarah recalled: "I think Salumet actually said this to us—they will show themselves when they know they will be accepted, otherwise there will be trouble."

This matter has been reported fairly fully, since it is clearly important that we see how such a remarkable conversation developed. The subject of wormholes was actually *introduced* into the discussion by our mind-linked ET friend from across the universe. And we were able to respond; this, thanks to Einstein and the endeavours of those brainstorming mathematicians of the mid-20th century.

It is very clearly evident from this sequence and from earlier exchanges that Bonniol and his group are conversant with much more that goes on in the universe than are those of us on Earth. But there remains a need for us to present to Bonniol the few facts that we *have* managed to gather together, so that he can add to those facts in some small measure for us. This modus operandi has been a recurring factor throughout our interplanetary conversations thus far. We have needed to make it clear that we have some small degree of awareness and understanding, such as it is, in order to make the most of these wonderful encounters with which we have been blessed.

So there is excellent evidence for wormholes as reality within creation and a configuration of the aether that should not be dismissed.

PART 5 - UNIVERSE CREATION

CHAPTER 14 – DATA FROM ANGELIC REALMS

Timing, as we have seen can be so important, and this may not be quite the *right* time to attempt to outline a full creation process; and furthermore of course, this is likely to be an impossible task for mere mortals. And yet I feel there have been a number of bold attempts and quite strong pointers towards some degree of understanding—so perhaps it would be an interesting exercise at least, to assemble the various pointers and see how well they connect with each other. After all, if the universe is 'steady state' and if it embodies the emergence of aether that suffuses all—with the conversion of that aether into matter, then there must be regions within the system where these essential processes are endlessly taking place. Reference has already been made to a large-scale cellular structure of the universe, and how these truly mega-cells of roughly 300 light-years diameter are void of galaxies. The evidence for expansion across the central cell zones suggests these regions would be zones favoured for aether-creation. I feel sure it is not quite as simple as that and there will be elaboration on this in due process. But firstly, it is appropriate that we elaborate regarding a treasure trove of

170

information received from spirit via the already mentioned at the start, Rev George Vale Owen very early in the 20th century, with all that material being published later in its entirety.

So who was the Rev George Vale Owen? He was Vicar of Orford, Lancashire, UK—a man devoted to his parishioners, and they referred to him affectionately as 'GVO'. His mother had passed to spirit in 1909, aged 63, and she began a series of communications with him from spirit in 1911. The communications from his mother, together with one from spirit named 'Astriel' may well have been a trial sequence to get things moving for GVO. If so, then it was a most successful trial and seems to have paved the way to higher things—to communications in fact from one known as 'Zabdiel', who is clearly from a higher level in spirit. And it was during our meeting of 12th May 2014 that I asked Salumet about Zabdiel, pointing out that much of what he had to say was in line with Salumet's own words to us—his reply:

~ **"He is one of the Angelic Group."**

I had responded: "Ah! He is Angelic!—he was mentioning *'cosmic energy'* as being more fundamental than the aether; and the process of creation involving both cosmic energy and the aether, and this leading to the material Creation. And I couldn't help thinking there is so much in line with your teaching in that."

To which Salumet then responded with the further comment:

~ "Yes, he still has a way to go, as we all do. But yes, when you speak of Creation you are speaking of *'prime energy'*. You are speaking of that Great Power who creates all things. And in creating the material worlds that he has—and I use *'he'* very dubiously—because he is *'energy'*, not a person— yes, all energy comes from the same source; whether it is to create universes or to create a planet such as Earth. You have to realise that no matter what you call it—cosmic energy—aether—it does not matter. To us, who have come some way, we recognise it only as the 'God Power'."

Well, that is quite a statement. I had not thought of Angels as *still having a way to go,* but of course we are all of us travelling together with the ever-ongoing creation—including its Angels—non-personalised energy or however we choose to regard them. It is again made clear that we speak of *primal energy* and not of beings, where those Angels are concerned. And there is further reference to that *cosmic energy*, first mentioned in chapter 12. I think the implication here, is that the cosmic energy is in one sense more fundamental than aether but they are so together in the part they play that we may use either word.

 I had added: "Yes, I felt that his medium was perhaps not quite a pure channel. He mentions *'Lords of Creation'*, as if there are actual beings responsible for the material creation."

~ "I believe if you look to the name it will give you something as to why that was voiced."

Paul: "—Because he was a *Reverend—*"

~ "Exactly so! So there is still a little moderation—a little input coming from the medium. There is still a reflection of the medium."

Salumet's channel is pure, since Eileen's consciousness is placed entirely to one side. [3]This is not so in the case of the reverend gentleman. The human mind can still moderate unless it is placed to one side. I had then suggested that the reverend gentleman's specific reference to 'Lords of Creation' was not quite right:

~ "Most of the time *their channelling* as you call it, is perfectly good, but always as I have said—there is always the risk of the human mind coming into play. There are no 'Lords of Creation'"

So there are no 'Lords of Creation'—that is now made perfectly clear. 'Their channelling' refers to that channelling by Zabdiel via Rev George Vale Owen. But there is much that is of immense value contained in the communications that

---

[3] Eileen is a 'FULL-TRANCE' medium, meaning she is in something like a sleep state when channelling Salumet and she has no recollection of what's been said afterwards. This allows for the clearest possible spiritual 'download', without human mind interference.

have since been published under the title: 'The Life Beyond the Veil', in four volumes: 'The Lowlands of Heaven', 'The Highlands of Heaven', 'The Ministry of Heaven' and 'The Battalions of Heaven'. The second volume: 'The Highlands of Heaven' [4], presents the Zabdiel material, and as Salumet says: most of the time their channelling is perfectly good. And several particularly interesting phrases concerning processes within the universe were included in the 2nd April 1919 communication. Zabdiel states quite clearly that spirit activates aether and aether activates matter. He indicates that Earth's chemists are beginning to become aware and, as he puts it, have reached the 'vestibule', but ahead of their understanding lies the 'temple', and then within the 'temple', the 'sanctuary'. The latter he describes as *the abode of spirit,* and only when scientists reach this will they realise *it to be the dynamo that energises aether, and through it, matter.* So Zabdiel makes it very clear that the energy route is:

Spirit > aether > matter

So we have words from two Angelic sources on the mode of creation, each delivered in rather different circumstance and separated by around one hundred years. Zabdiel is quick to point out that this is not to be seen as a fully automatic process. There is a will/personality direction of the energy involved, of matter of all things on Earth is influenced by spirit entities both incarnate and discarnate; so one might

174

say: the quality of creation is influenced by minds—by the minds of humans both past and present.

There was one occasion when Zabdiel wished to illustrate a problem that can sometimes arise for spirit workers whilst working in the various spirit realms, and this illustration involved a most intriguing proposition:

~ **"If you were to endeavour to build up a machine for the manufacture of aether, and the conversion of it into matter, you would find no substance to your hand on Earth of sufficient sublimity to hold the aether, which is of a force greater and more terrific than any force which is imprisoned within what you understand as matter."**

So this is consistent with the aether being extremely powerful and I think we may assume that its conversion to matter requires far more stringent conditions than would be to hand on the physical Earth or indeed on any other planet that we might care to imagine. Towards the end of that earlier meeting with Salumet of 28th March 1995, Leslie had chanced to observe that our minds just cannot think beyond the speed of light and our teacher had responded:

~ **"Yes. What you cannot comprehend, is that there is so much more that is not available to you, but of course is there. It is there and although your scientists work hard to** try to explain many of these things, their knowledge is too limited—too limited."

That was then. Moving on 17-years to 30th July 2012, Salumet was saying:

~ **"There are many energy waves that mankind has yet to discover. There is a continuance of discovery ahead for your scientists—energy waves they have not as yet discovered."**

It was then made clear that this would be *new discovery* and not *re*-discovery, so far as Earth is concerned, but those same energy waves have in fact been known and utilised by ET-visitors *to* our planet. As Salumet withdrew, another joined us speaking via Sarah. He explained:

~ *"I am most interested in your scientists, and I heard your master speak of the new energies that you will discover. And I just wanted to say to you that this is something that I am most interested in, and I'm trying to impress upon your scientists one of the energies that is available to you now. But it is not easy, and I hope that I will be able to continue with my work so that you as a people will be able to go very much further in your thinking and your development."*

I declared this to be much needed and inquired if our visitor had himself been a scientist in Earth life:

~ "I was, yes indeed, I was. But of course, the knowledge was very much limited at that time. But I've always felt there was something that I could not put my finger on, and now that I have returned to spirit I realise it was the help I was getting from spirit. So you see, I have in turn decided: this is my job now—to try to influence those scientists who are at present working so hard—though may I say: a little bit in the wrong direction? But it will come—I know it will come; but it just needs a little—tweaking, shall we say in the middle—so as to turn their thinking a little bit to the other direction. And then I will be able to influence them very much more."

Well perhaps it is interesting to see how our efforts are viewed by those in spirit who are a little more understanding of the problems, and who can see that little bit more clearly what is needed. I made reference to 'aether' and its current fashionable name of 'Higg's Field' or 'Higg's Ocean'. I was delighted to learn that our visitor actually had knowledge of the CERN particle accelerator but he declared that team not to be the group of his particular interest; adding that that group is indeed learning much from its own efforts. He went on to explain that he is influencing others who sit in the background scratching their heads, wondering in which direction they should now go. They are, it seems, aware of a need to change their thinking—a useful step in the right direction perhaps. So maybe Big Bang theory is at last about to be abandoned by the mainstream and be replaced by a more realistic thought pattern, but all this is very new

Let us now return to Zabdiel's idea of building a machine for the manufacture of aether. One has of course to see such a project as an outrageous notion—at least, as an *Earthly* proposition it would be without doubt a non-starter. But quite obviously, there have to be locations in the universe where aether *is indeed manufactured*—that has to be. So where are those locations? And what criteria would we expect for those *matter*-producing locations? Well, firstly aether would be drawn into the zones where 'matter manufacturing' occurs, and probably at a very much faster pace than would be required for mere matter-upkeep. Secondly, matter occurs throughout the universe in quite large discrete clusters called 'galaxies'. The general format of galaxies suggests that they mostly spiral outwards from a central region. One might therefore consider matter-production to be fairly central within the galactic unit. And today's astronomers know that what are termed 'super-massive black holes' occur in galactic centres. So a question we might ask ourselves is: why is a black hole black? The simple answer is: because light does not escape from it—hence it appears to us black. Yes, but why should that be? Does the blackness relate to the speed at which aether is being drawn into the black hole? Theory has named the critical shell from which light cannot escape as the 'event horizon'. Now let us suppose that having reached the event horizon, aether is now travelling at *the speed of light*. If light's medium is travelling at the speed of light into the super-massive black hole (SMBH); that would of course explain why light does not escape—that would explain why a SMBH appears black. And the huge unimaginable gravitational energy of a SMBH would be the power source that draws aether and whatever else and drives the process. Another question to ask ourselves is: why do galaxies have the spiral form? Well, if aether really is being swallowed up at the speed of light, one might easily compare it to 'water going down the plughole'—it forms a whirlpool. So we have the basis for an explanation of the spiral form of galaxies; also for the reason why there are SMBHs at galactic centres. And for a rational explanation of galaxy formation one has to recognize aether as having a key role in the process. But what happens to all that aether that is drawn into the SMBH? Well, my guess is: it transmutes into matter to be ejected as a nebulous cloud of matter having star-forming potential. Stars can then form from this cloud in the galaxy central region, when the time is right.

During our conversation of 24th September 2012, Salumet made it very clear that the aether is *part of all creation* and added the fact that *it is able to change*. It is therefore appropriate that in our theories we see aether as playing a major role in universe creation and in the ongoing universe format. And as a general principle, our teacher has always encouraged us to think simply—as does the child—to go within and seek answers to questions that arise. I sometimes feel that our scientists are over-complicating matters when they delve into higher mathematical excursion, and it is so easy to get carried away with complexity of thought construction and lose sight of the essential reality. And today's pattern of professional institutions with their associated peer-reviewed journals that has built up, seems to be promoting complexity of detail and adherence to themes that are currently fashionable. This might well be viewed as a problem to be overcome. One nevertheless has to admire the dedication that has gone into scientific research over the years—even if, as the above visitor from spirit has indicated: the thinking needs to be turned a little bit in the other direction! But even research that heads in the wrong direction can often help in the end to point out a reasoned way forward and to reveal a proper direction for reality.

CHAPTER 15 – NEBULAE AND STAR NURSERIES

So just what exactly do we mean by a nebula? The word derives from Latin meaning 'cloud'; but a cloud of what? Well, in the cosmological sense it is an extremely extensive cloud of gas and dust, and its composition and temperature will vary enormously across cosmic time; this since it is a precursor to much that is to follow. And what is to follow will lead eventually to the formation of new suns, new planets and new solar systems. Modern astronomers are to be congratulated, in that they have made enormous strides in recent years, in their mapping of the heavens and in making deductions; so much so that a number of things at last show signs of falling into place. Nebulae appear to us, viewed of course from vast distance, as 'objects' in the night sky possessing unmistakable beauty of colour and form. But perhaps 'object' is the wrong word to use for a diffuse cloud that we can only observe from afar. Nebulae are extensive and often wispy in outline. Astronomers in fact measure their spread across the heavens in light-years, so by our standards they are of truly breath-taking size and format.

Improved astronomical equipment has added in no small measure to recent progress. That equipment includes the

Hubble space telescope launched in low Earth orbit in 1990. This has provided excellent and much improved images that are without the inconvenience of Earth's atmospheric distortions; so that much clearer well-defined photographs are now available that reveal details as seen from *beyond* our atmosphere. And since our own Milky Way galactic centre is hidden from view if we rely only upon the light normally visible to our eyes, what is termed 'low frequency array' (LOFAR) has now been developed, enabling the galactic centre to be viewed—using other quite different wavelengths. So our galactic centre can now be studied in useful detail by means of radio frequencies of 330 and 74 megahertz. And the source designated 'Sgt A' has been identified as one huge Black Hole having a mass millions of times greater than our sun. There are also galactic central regions that contain hot young stars heating the gases that surround. So it would appear that the nebulae represent a significant stage in universe creation, as might be expected. And nebulae provide the elements from which new stars and new solar systems are then able to develop. Their colours relate to the chemical elements that are present—predominantly the simpler elements. Nebulae frequently contain around 90% hydrogen, 10% helium and only 0.1% of the heavier elements. They have extensive spread, their sizes varying enormously, so that, as stated, their span is measured in light-years. They have been classified according to appearance and to their known or deduced detail:

Emission Nebulae: These are gas clouds of high temperature, within which a star energises the atoms with an ultraviolet radiation. The energised atoms then fallback into lower energy states. This causes a nebula to glow. Nebulae mostly glow red, simply because this is the colour produced by hydrogen and hydrogen is usually present in abundance.

Reflection Nebulae: These nebulae are different in that they do not generate their own radiation. They are clouds of dust and gas that reflect the light produced by a *nearby* star or group of stars. They are frequently the sites of new star formation and they usually appear blue; this on account of the way the light gets scattered.

Dark Nebulae: Dark Nebulae or Absorption Nebulae are similar to Reflection Nebulae in their composition, but are illuminated from behind. It is simply the back-lighting that is responsible for their dark appearance. They are of common occurrence, and in fact occupy roughly 2% of our night sky. Some are visible to the unaided eye, for example: that known as the Coal-sack Nebula, in the direction of Centaurus and Southern Cross.

Nebulae—The General Details: Whilst several nebulae may be seen with the unaided eye, more become visible using a good pair of binoculars. A telescope is required to display fine detail. But even when aided by a telescope, the eye is insufficiently sensitive to reveal the subtleties of colour. Photographic procedures are useful here—especially using the more recently developed digital photography. The digital camera has led to surprising innovations, and not only in astronomy. (These cameras are also able to reveal the 'energy orbs' that are present in spiritual locations!) But, in astronomy, digital photography can reveal the often very beautiful colour detail of nebulae. And the Hubble space telescope is now revealing so much—views of nebulae that could not be observed from Earth prior to its launch. And so, astronomers now know of zones of active star formation within many galaxies that were previously thought of as simply inert. M42, the Orion nebula is a bright emission nebula, easily visible to the unaided eye and illuminated by a group of young stars at its centre. It is quite extensive and measures more than thirty light-years across. M8, the Lagoon nebula is bigger, extending to more than 150 light-years across. M20, the Trifid nebula, a refection nebula, is more colourful. It has a diversity of elements responsible for shades of red, blue and pink, while dark streams of dust divide it into three distinct zones—hence its name: the Trifid nebula.

Stella Nurseries: It is the opinion of cosmologists that nebulae may remain seemingly dormant for millions of years before star-formation becomes possible. Then gravity from a passing star or perhaps a shock wave of some kind may initiate a disturbance that can promote star formation. The beginning of this process would be marked by a coalescence of dust/matter to form clumps. These clumps then develop—become larger, and of course this means that their gravity also increases. Gravity attracts more and more matter so that there is further size increase until one or more clumps becomes a proto-star. As proto-stars continue to enlarge, gravity becomes much more highly significant—compressing interior so that temperature rises—temperatures being raised perhaps to levels wildly beyond any human imagination. Should a temperature of 18 million degrees be reached, then nuclear fusion will be triggered. Nuclear fusion is the key factor that marks the birth of a new star. It is the nuclear fusion process that makes a star a star. The fusion process involves just the lighter elements— two hydrogen nuclei will unite to produce one helium nucleus plus energy as the main ongoing initial process that then continues for millions of years (so in Mendeleev's Periodic Table, element no. 1becomes element no. 2 in the ongoing process). Nuclear fusion accompanied by prodigious energy release is the normal solar function as is so with our own sun. During the early stage of star formation, solar wind will clear away excess gas and dust, while smaller nearby aggregates of matter might well form into planets. Thus, we have the formation of a new solar system. Several stellar nurseries are currently known to astronomers. [Nuclear fusion, as a significant step in the creation process, is a different process from nuclear fission—the splitting of a *large* atom with release of energy.] These details are the observed and conjectured *physical* factors involved in star nursery development. Since non-material factors are currently ignored by mainstream scientists, their influence has not at this point in time been considered. The trigger for star formation (and probably much else) is of course likely to relate to non-material criteria rather than have to wait for the chance passing of a star or shock wave.

The discoveries continue and our teacher keeps us informed of some. On 19th January 2015, Salumet was saying:

185

~ **"I would also like to say to you this evening that you will become aware this year of your time, of new finds—within 'the heavens' as you call them—the planets and the stars. There will be information forthcoming, of new stars within your own galaxy."**

Serena wished to know if those discoveries would have an impact upon us. Salumet affirmed simply that they would be noticed; also that they are not really *new* stars but just previously unobserved ones. It was the very next day that I came across an article on the Internet, also dated 19th January 2015, describing the discovery of two new planets within what is termed the 'Goldilocks zone' of their own star systems; that should have favourable life-support conditions—coincidence? What astronomers call the Goldilocks zone is that part of a star system that has conditions somewhat similar to Earth—temperature such that water will neither be substantially evaporated nor be permanently frozen—a 'comfort zone' as Earth-dwellers might see it. The two freshly observed planets, designated Kepler 438b and Kepler 442b, are also of quite similar size and orbit times to our own planet. There has also been mention of a 3-star system forming within a dense gas filament. So it seems that discoveries are coming thick and fast, helped enormously by the Hubble space telescope and LOFAR explorations.

It has been claimed that the hypothetical singularity followed by the hypothetical Big Bang—each derives from Einstein's

General Relativity. But this claim of course contravenes his statement made in that 1920 lecture. And so, one cannot but help entertain the feeling, that singularity and Big Bang would be rather unlikely to issue directly from the great man's work. That is why the much more recent work of Ahmed Farag Ali and Saurya Das should be of interest. Their work takes into account an investigation in the 1950s by the theoretical physicist David Bohm. Bohm had set about the task of replacing 'classical geodesics' (shortest distance between two points on a curved surface) with what is termed 'quantum trajectories'. Ali and Das have substituted Bohm's quantum trajectories into equations by Amal Kumar Raychaudhuri and Alexander Friedmann. It was Friedmann, who in 1922 had established a set of equations describing space expansion, these having been derived from the field equations of General Relativity. So this is how General Relativity came to be linked to Big Bang and singularity theory. But the subtlety of this new work lies in the fact that the classical geodesics can eventually cross one another while Bohm's quantum trajectories cannot do this. And without any crossing point, the adjusted equations do not indicate a singularity or Big Bang. The equation adjustment also leads to recognition of infinite time—the same as saying the universe has no beginning and no end. And the scientists also point out that, within cosmology, the quantum trajectory substitutions could conceivably be seen as a 'cosmological constant'. All this feels much more comfortable to accept, aligning as it does to known spiritual input, a steady state universe and with General Relativity, the outcomes of which are upheld. The work described even adds substance to Einstein's cosmological constant, which he had felt obliged to introduce.

Nebulae clearly feature as a highly significant physical step in the endless creation process, whilst a huge amount of work has been involved through the last century in arriving at this conclusion. And the brainstorming continues at ever increasing pace, aided by more recent technological advances.

CHAPTER 16 – THE MATTER-ANTIMATTER DUALITY

Rugerro Santilli was Italian born and studied physics at the University of Naples, then on to Turin. He became a visiting scholar to the mathematics department at Harvard. He conducted research financed by NASA and became Associate Professor of Physics at Boston University, this leading to U.S. citizenship. He went on to found several institutions of which he was lead scientist. Santilli came to be highly regarded in mathematics, physics and cosmology, and was actually nominated for Nobel Prize in physics and chemistry—all very commendable and readily admired by the scientific fraternity of that period.

A more recent achievement has been the development of a telescope, which differs markedly from the Galileo telescope in that it is not based on convex lenses. It is instead based on *concave* lenses, and Santilli has given his name to it—the Santilli telescope[5]. His object has been to observe the light of antimatter out there in the universe having a negative refractive index, his belief being that concave lenses are required in order to focus that light. This previously unknown instrument involving a previously unknown principle represent of course huge departures from the standard way of scientific thinking, so much so that he is now regarded by many as a 'fringe scientist'.

Until this development—that all that exists in the heavens can be seen by our eyes and by our optical instruments had been a comfortable backwater in which humans had basked; so much so that such a concept would be seen as one huge step away from that longstanding belief. Santilli feels, as do increasing numbers today, that there is in effect, the intention to suppress or simply have no interest in new departures that could conflict with that well entrenched scientific theory of past and present, even when that theory is wrong. But this departure story does not end here.

One evening over Tampa Bay, Florida, Santilli was working with a paired Galileo and a Santilli telescope, when cloud prevented a clear view of the heavens. On lowering the instruments, he was surprised to find that clearly visible entities appeared on the camera screen of the Santilli telescope. These were invisible to the eye; neither did they appear on the camera screen of the Galileo telescope. This led to his developing a method, using the pair of telescopes to search for entities within Earthly environment, and some of these entities have been seen to exhibit intelligent movement. This of course can only endorse that view of him as a fringe scientist. Perhaps we might compare him to Nikola Tesla, whose genius has remained obscure for quite well into the future.

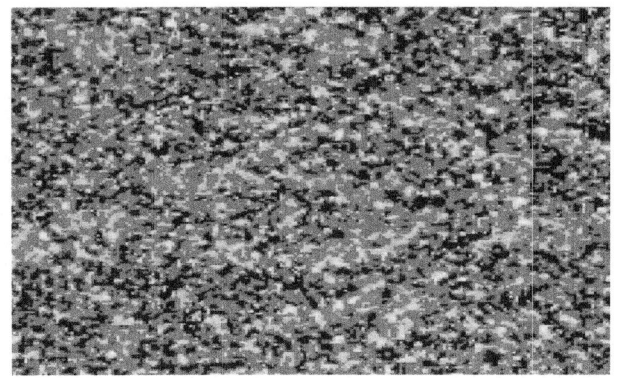

The photo was taken using paired Santilli and Galileo telescopes as shown:

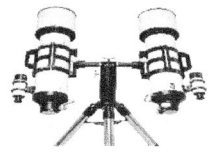

So how does this relate to 'matter-antimatter duality? It is a fact that our present scientific community is well aware that in the universe, in relation to their theories, much still remains missing. And Salumet (8th February 2016) has commented as follows:

~ **"If there is matter, there is always antimatter. Yes, you always have to have a balance."**

So that really puts it in a nutshell. The two have to be created simultaneously.

And in a nutshell is where George's manuscript finished, though a final chapter had been planned, based upon a subsequent session with Salumet. The session is presented in full below, so that the reader can get a taste of what a Salumet Circle meeting is like, with the usual deep spiritual questions. You may then like to draw your own conclusions about the Aether and it's place in the Multiverse:

16*th* May 2016
George: Good evening Salumet and welcome to you.

~"**Good evening.**"

All: Good evening.

~"**It gladdens us all when we see such dedication as you provide within this room. I would this time, my dear friends, just say to you that however you feel about the state of your world at this time, and it would seem that there is always strife—I want to still reassure you that we are doing all that we can to bring Love and Peace to all people. We do not wish you to become despondent, because that would not help any situation. So be reassured, my dear friends, that with your help and the help of many others in this world, we will come at some stage to a more natural and loving situation here.**"

Paul: Thank you—yes, I think there are positive little ripples and signs. It's slow, but it's slowly changing.

~"**Yes, and that is what we still need to do—to have positive attitudes—all of you. I would wish to just say to you this time that even your scientific world is changing**"

192

slowly, that their doubts are a little less than they were ten of your years ago. So in this respect it is a good sign that there are changes happening."

George: We have recently spoken of the 'Santilli telescope' and the observation of an anti-matter universe **(yes)**. You suggested I might think further on this matter **(yes)**. Well, my physical thinking is like this: The aether plus its mode of transmission governs the *speed of light* to this planet. Its mode of transmission has been described as torsional or twisting, and this controls the speed of light until it strikes matter and transfers its energy to that. And thinking physically on this, if we consider a single twist, if it goes further to a *break point*, it will produce a clockwise part and an anti-clockwise part, which might suggest matter and anti-matter. Anyway, the aether represents a stage in the production—the creation of matter, and there seems to be good evidence for an anti-matter universe. And the present scientific community is aware and acknowledges that their reasoning leaves a large part of the universe unaccounted for. The anti-matter universe would contribute to that part which is not at the moment acknowledged. I would be glad of any further commentary you might have on that Salumet.

~"Yes, I understand what you are saying, but to simplify it for the others, it is not as complicated as it may seem. There will never be a full understanding with your scientific world, but it indicates to us how much knowledge they are beginning to gain. Always I have told you there is plus and minus in all parts of life, and this applies to the matter of the universe and the universes further afield. Of course, I would say that your scientists are dealing very well with the information which is being fed to them from our world. That is the first step I have to make to you.

They would have no knowledge at all if some of it was not coming from us. You know and understand that all of your life is dependent upon being spiritual beings. And when you speak of the aether—of course, it is the most important part in gauging how the rest of the universes work. But I feel for this time, your scientists need to remain uncomplicated with their visions—and allow more knowledge to come from us, which would then gain *them* more knowledge, here on this Earth."

George: Yes, and it would speed this process up if more of them went within.

~"Yes, and listened to that still voice; yes of course it would help, but although in times past I have said almost they are a little ignorant of all that is happening. We have now reached a stage where some of them are beginning to listen—to work out for themselves that information and to define what it is all about. But they will never have the full answer, not whilst you remain upon this Earth plane."

George: Yes, and would you agree that the aether plays a major role?

~"It is a natural role—it is not something that is *made*, it has always been."

George: Yes, it plays a major role in the Creation (yes) and a major role in—

~"existence."

George: Yes, and in controlling the speed of light.

194

~"And that also, yes, I would agree with you on that one point. Does that help you?"

George: That clarifies very nicely, thank you.

~"I hope that the others have understood, because you are a gentleman of much wisdom, but it is not always easy for the others to fully understand your questions, but we are grateful for them."

George: Well thank you—I'm writing this book on the aether **(yes)**, and it may well be that it will be beyond a few people, but I hope that some will find it of interest.

~"Yes, we can assure you there will be interest. *(Thanks)* We thank you, my dear friend, we thank you for all the good work that you have done—the words that you have printed, and many people have come to know just a little more of the life that continues."

Mark: I believe you told us over a year ago about the discovery of more planets and that's come to fruition—they announced that about a week ago.

~"Yes, I am always happy to hear that our information materialises for you, and that you know that the words that I give to you are made of truth—we thank you for that."

Serena: Could I ask a question slightly related to George I believe, about Adamantine Particles **(Yes)**. What are they?

~"What are they? They are made from the substance of all life—if that is a simple answer for you."

195

Serena: Because they're very, very, *very* small, aren't they?

~"Minute, I would say—is the word that I would use. Yes, they are part of existence. I do not know how else to explain it to you—yes."

George: We respect that what comes to us from you Salumet, is truth **(yes)**. The generation of that truth, one could almost say, is a 'feedback process' from all knowledge that has been gained from this and other planets in the universe **(yes)** and other univer*s*es, I believe you have said in the past.

~"Well you see—*all* of your world is never still. It is evolving in the same way as you are, and mankind is a curious creature. He forever seeks answers to many things. Sometimes these questions are irrelevant to your spiritual growth, but we understand that, because of the curiosity, you like to ask more and more questions. The question, my dear friends, I would wish you to ask is: how do we become more spiritual whilst in the human body? That is the important question. Do you understand?"[4]

---

[4] *Salumet widens the discussion here, suggesting that pondering such subjects as the Aether is fine, but it would be better to spend more time going within, unlocking the secrets of the Mind. Salumet has told us that the Power of Thought is the most powerful thing we possess explaining how this power was better understood by so-called ancients. So it could be more rational and constructive to turn our attention inwards and the best way to do this is in Meditation, a subject comprehensively explained by Salumet—see website.*

Natalie: On that note, at the beginning of the year, I had an experience in this room that I hadn't felt before—like I wasn't here **(yes)**. Like my heart was bursting out of my chest, and I felt like I was being pulled back somewhere and it was weird, it's like I could just about hear, in the distance, someone in the room like I wasn't quite here, but I was here. I wondered if you could clear that up?

~"Yes, it was part of your development, it is part of the Spirit separating from the body; and we know you found it a little uncomfortable at the time. So we try never to— what is the word you would use—to *hold* that someone would feel uncomfortable? But indeed, it was another step in your own development." *(Thanks)*

George: I guess the main thing is a going *within* to see what we can receive—but exercises such as we had last week would also help to develop this. *(Referring to last week's self-development exercise to develop clairvoyance.)*

~"It would help each one of you to develop in your own individual ways. After all, you are each individuals and although you come together in Love and Peace, in your daily lives you are very different, but that makes no difference to the Spirit; so yes, you must go within if you wish to be in more contact with the Spirit. I find sometimes it difficult to explain that you are all *ONE* at the moment. You *are* Spirit and yet you have this human body, which sometimes causes you and your minds to become a little cluttered. So when you go within, the Spirit becomes freer. That is the time that as individuals, you should ask your questions, and you will receive your answers—maybe not exactly what you want to hear, but still it is your own spiritual answer."

197

George: And I think I would be right in saying that you Salumet are part of that *oneness*, because you receive so much from everywhere and recycle it.

~"Ah, that is a very good way to put it. I have never been called a *'recycling bin'!*

(Hearty laughter)

So I will remember that my dear friends, yes—Recycling—I must remember..."

(More ripples of laughter)

George: But do you regard yourself as part of that *oneness*?

~"I do. I am part of many parts that is a whole. And again, we are going to a subject which is a little complicated for the human mind. But yes you know, and I told you from the very beginning that I speak as a conglomerate of beings, and that is still true today."

George: So can we see a conglomerate of beings as...

~"You can see a conglomerate of being as a *Universe of Truth*—the University of Truth, if you like."

George: —A collection of parts, or is that putting it a bit too physically?

~"I think for understanding that is a good way to put it—yes—yes, and parts which have never existed as

humankind, and parts which *have* existed; but as a whole we are just bound in *Love* and *Existence*."

George: You say 'and parts that *have existed*'?

~"**In some form—yes, have existed in some form. But again, what is important is the *Truth* that we bring to you. I hope that is helping you.**"

Paul: Yes, it widens the picture a little more, and I just had the thought: maybe it helps the whole Truth that you are a conglomerate with formless beings and those that have *had* form, that no longer have form—

~"**Yes, but not form as you would understand. That is why I say it is more complicated than words can say.**"

Paul: Right—so they wouldn't have been human.

~"**No.**"

Paul: But yes—some form—it gives us something to think on.

~"**It is something for you to consider—yes.**"

George: Would any of those forms be physical?

~"**No.**"

Ben: When we pass to Spirit, we sometimes take on a *form* of how we looked when we were on the Earth I believe—for recognition purposes. **(Yes)** So when we pass to Spirit and if we were to call upon you for a conversation, how would you appear to us?

~"I can take—I can be transformed to the form of a human in order to teach on the lower levels, but I only come so far, so often. There are many teachers in our world who are prepared to teach those who have questions. It is not something that I do with regularity, but if you were to call upon me whilst in Spirit, you would find that your answers will come. (Thanks) There are many teachers in Spirit and there is much you can learn when first you take your place there. But the others understand this, do you not?"

Paul: Sort of—I think, in the sense that there are vast libraries and teachers; and you *know* that the Truth is *there*, as opposed to on the Earth where—*(finding truth can be tricky)*

~"You will no longer doubt the Truth once you have returned to Spirit. After all my dear friend, you are returning *Home.* Nothing will seem strange, *(Agreed)* so all will seem familiar and you will feel boundless Love— *Unlimited Love.*"

Paul: Yeah, I guess it's like you get beautiful days on the Earth, but that's not the norm usually, but they're probably just small compared to in Spirit.

~"Yes, I would say that in comparison, a beautiful day here would seem very hazy in Spirit. It would seem dull, although, as human beings, you would think it a most beautiful day. The colours—everything about Spirit is—I don't know how to explain it to you properly. I can only say the beauty will astound you."

Paul: Yes, I think we get the gist, but until we experience it *again,* we won't know for sure.

George: Perhaps we should think in terms of a beautiful summer's day here being a less-than-halfway stage in beauty?

~"Yes, although it is beautiful to human beings, to us it seems a little dull—yes you are correct—yes."

Paul: And yet, for many, even though the learning can occur as you say, on that side *(in Spirit world)* many will choose to come back. *(to Earth plane)—why* would you choose to come back to the very hazy place *(Planet Earth)* at the best of times? But I suppose you do get the *focus* for certain lessons perhaps—

~"Yes, always the choice remains with the Spirit. Of course, some are not quite so keen to return too quickly, but that is their free will and that is always respected. But there is advice from those teachers in our world who will offer guidance and Love. And let me say to you all, my dear friends: you never return to a lifetime unless the decision has been made by *you*. So never feel that it is something that you *must* do—it is something that you have decided is right for the growth of your Spirit. And after all, that is what these lives are about—the growth of your Spirit and returning *Home*."

George: Yes, it is a growth of Spirit and not a retrograde step!

~"Yes. No, you must never look upon it as that."

Ben: Would we have the chance to reincarnate onto a different planet, or will we always be human when we reincarnate?

~"There is much discussion about this that you can return—energy can be transmuted, but I would say: no, you will not do that. You will not inhabit another planet in that form. And I know there is dispute about this, but that is my answer to you."

George: You said at some stage that a new energy would be forthcoming from the sea (yes). One gentleman seems to have worked out a process for making alcohol out of seaweed, but I don't think that's what you had in mind.

~"Well, I thank you for the information, but no I was speaking of benefits to mankind in general and not seaweed drink. Although I must say that the seaweed in your seas can be beneficial—yes. But there are many things happening in your world. As I say: people, although it may seem that all is going wrong, it is not my friend, it is almost like a *cleansing*—a cleansing of the Soul in order for you all to move forward."

Paul: Ah, that's a lovely way of looking at it. It does feel like that—this year and the last few years.

~"Those of you who are sensitive to Spirit would see the difference, although many people with negative thoughts would see only the 'unhappiness', the 'wars'—the negative stuff in your world. But keep positive my dear friends— keep positive on all matters."

Paul: Yes, it's like a detox—you have to get rid of all this stuff, but you have to get it out first, so it's coming out, isn't it? (Yes)—we're seeing it in the media.

~"The more 'sensitives' we have, the better the understanding will become. So I leave that all with you, my dear friends, and hope that it has given you a little food for thought."

George: Yes indeed! I feel this has been a wonderful evening, which has taken us further forward and I'm sure it will be of great interest to many of our readers **(yes)**, thank you Salumet.

~"I thank all of you my dear friends, I thank you all for your Love, for your dedication and I wish you could see the growth of your own Spirits since first we met—you would be surprised.
So I leave you now, cloaked in my Love and in the Love of those here in my world, until we meet once more."

George: And we send our Love to you all in your world—thank you.
Thanks and farewells

George's meeting notes:
1: *Matter and anti-matter:* *What follows is intended to bring the more general reader up to an understanding of that technical question to Salumet concerning matter and anti-matter. This follows a first mention of the Santilli telescope in a question to Salumet on 8th February. Salumet's statement at that time was: 'I would only say this to you, my dear friends: if there is matter, there is always anti-matter—you always have to have a balance.' This is the invention of Dr Rugerro Santilli that actually reveals (and proves the existence of) an anti-matter universe. So it should help the general reader enormously if we begin by considering the nature of waves, beginning with water waves:*

Waves on water: *We are all familiar with ocean waves. They are clearly visible, they travel slowly and they have their energy, which they give up on reaching a coastline. This energy transfer is apparent when we see shifting sands and cliff erosion.*

Sound waves in air: *This is a compression wave with alternate compressed and reduced pressure parts. Sound waves travel very much faster than water waves—around 340 metres per second (but with dependence on temperature, humidity etc). Just like water waves, sound has energy which is given up when it strikes a surface. If that surface happens to be our eardrum, then it vibrates the eardrum and that is the basis of our hearing ability. It is possible for extremely loud sounds to knock down walls and to shake machines to pieces. So in these cases, the energy transfer is well demonstrated. We must bear in mind that both water wave and sound waves are entirely physical involving physical media through which they travel.*

Light waves in the aether: *Light waves are very, very much faster again than sound waves—almost 300 million metres per second (186,000 miles per second). A reason for this is that the aether is non-physical so that the travelling light wave has no weight to shift. An important thing is that just like sound waves one can see it as units comprising pressure and reduced pressure parts—or each part may be a twist (torsion)—and Professor Ervin Laszlo makes a strong case for this—or it may be both. But whatever the structure of the light wave, the important thing for us to observe is that just like water waves and sound waves, it carries energy which transfers to the surface that it falls upon. When that surface is our skin, it produces sunburn. When that surface is dark, the absorbed energy makes it hot. Lighter surfaces reflect more energy and that is why sunhats are usually white; so all these waves have the common feature of carrying energy that is*

*given up on reaching a material surface, and the
understanding of one type of wave should help us to visualise
another.*

The aether: *The aether is a universal (non-physical) essence
that has several functions: (1) It conveys sunlight and starlight
to this and other planets. (2) It sustains life on this and other
planets. (3) Aether has an essential role in the creation
process—a half-way stage between spirit and matter. (4)
Matter and anti-matter are produced simultaneously, and
there have been several references to the fact that this is so.
These details lead to the conclusion that there is indeed an
anti-matter universe. This is claimed by Dr Rerrero Santilli
and is confirmed by Salumet.*

~~~~~~

*There is always more that could be said and the work of the
dedicated Salumet Circle continues. The audios and
transcripts are all freely available on the websites mentioned
in the references. It was understood from the beginning that
the expansive knowledge offered by Salumet, needs to be
shared with the world:*

*Of course, George's journey continues and he still visits the
Salumet Circle. In fact, Salumet confirmed the following on
10ᵗʰ October 2016:*

~ **"I wish to say to all of you that our dear friend, and we
are aware of his loss to you, he has arrived *Home* safely.
And having the inquisitive mind that he had, he is now
beginning to seek for some answers.** *(Smiles)* **This I know**

would not be news for you, but I wish you to know that there are so many on our side of life who will keep him 'engaged', shall we say, for some time. He has expressed a desire to meet with the other gentleman who started this group. *(Leslie Bone)* Of course, if that is his desire, then that will be so. And of course to meet with family and friends again is just wonderful to him. He may not come to you directly himself, but he may use his voice through another for a short time; so be aware of this."

There have been plenty of clairvoyant communications since, including this memorable vision via Eileen, on 2020/03/02: Eileen was seeing dear George sitting happily on a pile of books—George loved books and had a fine collection. He wanted to let us all know that he wished to speak, but that the time wasn't right. Paul suggested the right time would come and Eileen saw George smiling and as if on a magic carpet, he rose on his pile of books and glided away…

Thank you George 22/11/1930 - 23/09/2016
And on a final note, George sometimes said that his spiritual journey began in 1989, in Palenque Mexico. Sneaking into the

Mayan ruins at night, he sat on top of an ancient pyramid-temple, above the jungle canopy, gazing out at the starlit sky. And the Universe gave him this message:

"It's okay to tinker with the mechanics of the Universe, like Einstein and Newton—but the most important thing in the Universe is LOVE."

APPENDIX

Three days after the returning to Spirit realm of George, (26th September 2016) a lovely gentle one spoke via Eileen. It seemed perfect that this evening's theme should be Beauty in Spirit. Perhaps this was an example of orchestrated Love from Spirit, helping to remind us of the wonderful journey our dear George was now taking:

Good evening.

Paul: Good evening.

Lilian: Can you tell us your name?

Miriam—I'm looking around—it's very quiet.

Agreed

Lilian: There's only 5 of us. We're just a very small group tonight. *(Yes)* It's quite unusual to be so small.

Yes. I like quietness—I've always liked quietness.

Lilian: Yes, I can agree with you there. Sometimes I like to be with people, but yeah, to be in the garden and quiet is very nice.

Do you speak to the garden people?

Lilian: I do forget—In fact I'm glad you've said that.

Why do you forget?

Lilian: Why indeed! I haven't got a very good memory. Though I *do* thank the flowers—especially when they've come to the end of their life and you know, thank them for the flowers that have been...

Yes; you've seen nothing yet!

Lilian: No.

There is a lot to see and flowers are some of the things that a lot of people are taken aback by; not only their beauty, but their scent—yes.

Lilian: Can you pick up their thoughts as well?

They dance! They sing! So yes, you should be able to know what is being said. It is almost—I believe you would say a **choir!**

Lilian: Amazing!

Have you ever stopped in a garden and wondered why? Or just enjoyed the peace? But when you hear the **flowers** *sing, it stops you in your tracks!*

Paul: That's a lovely reminder for us to spend more time in our gardens.

Yes and the flowers are never separated in our world—never apart—always mixed.

Mark: Like a meadow...

That is good yes. Meadows in your world have their own significant song. Did you know that?

Mark: No—they have a much more sort of...

...Basic sound.

Mark: Yes, because they're allowed to form more naturally without so much human interference. *...interference yes.*

Lilian: I've just had a thought, can they communicate with bees, flies and so on?

Everything that is living has the ability to communicate, yes. That is why when you walk in a beautiful garden your spirits rise and you feel so good. So imagine when you come over here, can you imagine how greater that joy is; to see the colours, the flowers, the singing, the swaying—everything...

Paul: And even in a winter garden in this country some things remain flowering and seem to be alive—they're always alive, but they're still in *flower* often.

The Great Creator has thought of everything. Yes of course, there is a different kind of beauty in your world in the winter time; but yes, you have all of those flowers too—it is a sight to behold and one that leaves people in awe.

Paul: We just need to have a little more time and to open ourselves a little more to these things, don't we?

You do, but you are doing well if you tend your gardens well here; you are at the beginning of a beautiful journey.

Sarah: I remember the one who comes through known as Salumet, he told us we should really look at the plants, look at the flowers, look inside them and just see the beauty in them—and it's absolutely true!

Yes, and speak to them, yes, and listen—listen.

Sarah: Yes, I hadn't thought about the listening part of it. *(Yes)* When you say they're singing, what are they actually doing? Are they singing?

I just say 'singing'—it is a vibration, a higher vibration than you would be aware of here; and the different vibrations together is the most beautiful thing you will encounter.

Paul: I remember when I was walking in a lot of nature on my own in New Zealand. I could sometimes clearly tune into some kind of—it was like a choir of Angels, you could say, singing. I wondered if it was coming from the river, but I couldn't say for sure where it was coming from, but I was walking along this river. There was some kind of wonderful orchestra of music and sound.

Yes and you were privileged to hear that in this world. That is why when you encounter beautiful quiet areas in your world that you should take the time and appreciate what they have to offer you, because it is indeed beautiful.

Sarah: I was actually watching a programme on the telly about the *singing sands (yes)* and they get so hot they start to move and then it creates this noise, but actually you can hear that, you don't have to be in trance to be able to hear it.

Yes, it's wonderful, isn't it?

Agreed

And the whole of your Nature on this planet is wonderful. (Agreed) And I'm afraid it's little appreciated by many.

Sarah: Mankind has done it's best to destroy it!

210

Yes, but there are those who work towards re-educating man; that is going on even now as I speak.

Paul: It feels like a battle sometimes between big corporations and those who are trying to protect wildlife—I hope we're winning—gradually persuading people.

Yes, good people such as yourselves, with insight can only help those of us from Spirit who wish to correct all of these wrongs. We try to influence as much as we can.

Sarah: You're doing a very good job, because we're beginning to talk a lot more about it now *(yes)* and things like the ivory trade—there is no point in killing these wonderful animals just for their tusks *(no)* and the general public is siding much more for the animals and against the people who are doing the trade.

Yes, it takes people some time to become aware of what is wrong and what is right. It does not mean they are bad people, only misinformed or misguided; but education is a wonderful thing.

Sarah: And also when people are very poor and struggling in life, you can appreciate that some of them do this because they just need something to live on...

Yes, they need just to be guided away from that form of self-survival. But yes of course, it is understandable why it has happened in the past, but once people become more educated there is no excuse—there is a limit to making excuses for people who do damage to others, not only human beings, but your animals. They are loved dearly in this world.

Yes, so it has been most pleasant to have a few words with you and I can assure you there is much—whenever your time may be, you will be amazed.

Paul: Mm you've inspired us and I'm sure you'll inspire others who listen and read these words.

Yes.

Sarah: Paul and Mark's father *(George)* has just passed to Spirit and he learned a lot from this group, from the ones that

211

came through and he was a keen gardener, so I'm sure he's thoroughly enjoying all the beauty!

There is so much beauty, not only plants, everything that you have on Earth is just multiplied. You cannot really imagine it until you see it, but I just wanted you to know that the peace and the quietness also benefits the wildlife—the plants and all of those things.

So I am going to say goodbye to you all and perhaps we can have another talk another time.

Enthusiastic agreement + thanks

REFERENCES:

George E Moss, *Earth's Cosmic Ascendancy – Spirit and Extraterrestrials Guide us through Times of Change and Challenge,* White Crow Books, Guildford, UK, (2014).

Bonniol, Salumet & George E Moss, *The Chronicles of Aerah – Mind-link Communications across the Universe,* Trafford Publishing, Victoria BC, Canada, (2009).

Frederick David Tombe, *The Aether and the Electric Sea,* Belfast, Northern Ireland, UK, (2006).
(2006)

Rev G Vale Owen, *The Life Beyond The Veil: The Highlands of Heaven: Spirit Messages Received and Set Down,* Thornton Butterworth, London, UK, (1926).

Ruggero Santilli, *Isodual Theory of Antimatter with Applications to Antigravity, Grand Unification and Cosmology,* Springer, (2006).

Useful links/books featuring the teachings of Salumet:

Tales of Love and Light along the journey Home— *Conversations with people who are 'dead', but don't know it yet. 2023—Paul E Moss https://amzn.eu/d/9G1BGrT* **Salumet: His Mission to Planet Earth** *...you are already on the pathway of Light. 2005 – George E Moss https://amzn.eu/d/f1Zl7ju*

The Chronicles of Aerah – *Mind-Link Communications across the Universe. 2009 – George E Moss https://amzn.eu/d/164qWc5*
Earth's Cosmic Ascendancy – *Spirit and Extraterrestrials guide us through Times of Change and Challenge. 2014 – George E Moss https://amzn.eu/d/8GInqN8*
A Smudge in Time. *2000 – George E Moss (George's first book, giving an alternative history of Science/the world, with commentary from Salumet. https://amzn.eu/d/9yHeYyt*

The *Salumet transcripts* are *freely available* and can be read from the beginning, allowing *the* development of *your own 'trail of understanding'* of the communications. www.salumetandfriends.org –*A chronologically organised Library of transcripts, audios and other trance-channellings.* www.salumet.org –*An A-Z of the teachings, arranged by subjects, allowing quicker access to the material.*

To see a rare filmed session of the Salumet Circle, here's a link: https://www.youtube.com/watch?v=1hBIXN3nwjs

Alternatively, use your phone to scan the QR code:

Printed in Great Britain
by Amazon

45948283R00119